Girardet

Finally, an English language compilation of recipes from one of the greatest chefs of the past century. Frédy Girardet has always been a source of inspiration to professional chefs; it is nice to know that—with the publication of this book—a new generation of home cooks will be motivated to reach greater culinary heights.

—DANIEL BOULUD

A Kirsty Melville Book

Ten Speed Press
P.O. Box 7123
Berkeley, California 94707
www.tenspeed.com

Distributed in Australia by Simon and Schuster Australia, in Canada by Ten Speed Press Canada, in
New Zealand by Southern Publishers Group, in South Africa by Real Books, in Southeast Asia by
Berkeley Books, and in the United Kingdom and Europe by Airlift Book Company.

Some of the recipes in this book include raw eggs, meat, or fish. When these foods are consumed raw,
there is always the risk that bacteria, which is killed by proper cooking, may be present. For this reason,
when serving these foods raw, always buy certified salmonella-free eggs and the freshest meat and fish
available from a reliable grocer, storing them in the refrigerator until they are served. Because of the health
risks associated with the consumption of bacteria that can be present in raw eggs, meat, and fish, these
foods should not be consumed by infants, small children, pregnant women, the elderly, or any people who
may be immunocompromised.

Library of Congress Cataloging-in-Publication Data on file with the publisher.

ISBN 1-58008-411-7

Jacket design by Betsy Stromberg
Logo design on the cover by Julien van der Wal
Typesetting for the English edition by Tasha Hall
Copyediting by Brigit Binns

First printing, 2002
Printed in Hong Kong

1 2 3 4 5 6 7 8 9 10—05 04 03 02 01

Girardet

RECIPES FROM A
MASTER OF FRENCH CUISINE

Frédy Girardet

Photography by Pierre-Michel Delessert

Ten Speed Press
Berkeley / Toronto

Joël Robuchon, Paul Bocuse, and Frédy Girardet

Contents

Frédy Girardet by Joël Robuchon

When I think of Frédy Girardet, one word immediately springs to mind—"exceptional." Even that most evocative word, however, cannot adequately sum up this remarkable man. Above all, Frédy is a loyal friend, a rare being, and a unique chef.

Throughout his prestigious career, he has always set an example of total honesty, refusing to follow fashionable culinary trends for the sake of it, while remaining innovative and ahead of the pack. For over twenty years, this wise, discreet man has been widely admired for the way he has practiced his art in a suburb of Lausanne. Thanks to him, Crissier is on the world map.

Frédy is an enlightened observer, a single-minded hard worker. He listens, watches, and understands, and has become a model of inspiration and thoroughness.

He is the king of chefs on this planet, whose intelligent cooking combines spontaneity with tremendous thought. Behind the apparent simplicity lies a constant quest for perfection. He has a passion for ingredients, and absolute respect for their textures and flavors. Some of the marriages he makes seem very bold, but they are always entirely harmonious.

To this day, Frédy remains *the* cook of the 20th century. He may have left his stoves, but he is still passionate about cooking, as this book proves. Whatever the recipe—Fine Velouté of Petits Pois with Frogs' Legs and Osetra Caviar; Steamed Bouchot Mussels with Clam Brochettes, White Wine and Green Onions; Golden Monkfish Tails with Sesame Seeds and Curried Winter Vegetables; Curried Shoulder of Lamb with Golden Raisins; or Pineapple and Fig Charlottes with Almond Milk Ice Cream; Wild Strawberry and Champagne Mousseline; Warm Baked Figs with Lime Syrup and Raspberry Coulis—all these recipes, chosen at random from the book, reflect the richness and variety of his cooking.

I told Frédy I was greatly honored when he asked me to write the preface to his book. He simply replied "this is just a tiny selection of the dishes we served at Crissier between 1982 and 1996. I have modified the recipes to make them more accessible, because, like you, I love to share my knowledge, and ensure that anyone can recreate my dishes."

The hundred or more of his recipes that I discovered in this book are a testament to the immense creative talent of this extraordinary chef—a worthy mouthpiece for the pure, honest cooking of this exceptional man.

Frédy Girardet by Catherine Michel

"This is an astonishing success story for Switzerland, a country that has traditionally been better known for its hotel-keeping than for its fine palate, whose aim has been to export head chefs to work in the kitchen brigades of palaces. He has the gastronomic world at his feet, the jet set at his table, the world's press at his door…And amidst all the clamor that surrounds famous men, Frédy Girardet, like Voltaire's Candide, says nothing, but simply cultivates his garden; that secret garden where he dreams his cook's dreams."

This was how we introduced Frédy twenty years ago, in the preface to his first book *La Cuisine Spontanée (Spontaneous Cooking)*. It was the autumn of 1982, and the somewhat skeptical French publisher had ordered a limited print run of the first edition. It sold out in a week, and it is still selling; so far, more than 100,000 copies have been sold—unheard of for a cookbook. In 2000, it sold 10,000 copies, eighteen years after it first appeared, and three years after Girardet retired!

As the years went by, his fame grew. His modesty, so close to pride, remained undiminished, his culinary imagination remained as fertile as ever, and his secret garden is still impenetrable, even to his closest friends.

Why, at the height of his glory, did he retire from the career he loved so passionately?

Why, when not forced by ill health or money problems, did he sell his restaurant at Crissier, that high temple of gastronomy, to join the common herd?

Why has it taken him so long to write a second book?

Why has he not resumed his career, when on his own admission, he has an overwhelming desire to do so?

There is no doubt about it; his secret garden remains impenetrable, and we can only rely on supposition. Perhaps, at the age of 60-plus, he is afraid that he will never again achieve his dream of perfection.

Whatever the reason in November 1996, the world lost its greatest chef when he retired, and the world's press paid him eloquent tributes. Leafing through his book of polyglot press cuttings, it is interesting to see that articles written in French are by no means the most numerous.

These are some of the key dates in his career:

1975	Gault-Millau Clé d'Or
1980	Chevalier du Mérit Agricole Français
1986	Entry in *Larousse Gastronomique*, and Chevalier de la Lion d'Honneur
1987	Chevalier de l'Ordre des Arts et des Lettres
1988	Sacré "Cuisinier du siècle" ("Cook of the century")
1989	Grand Prix International de l'Art de la Cusine
1994	Three stars in the first Michelin Red Guide to Switzerland, and Médaille d'Or de la Ville de Lausanne
1998	Olympic Order conferred by the IOC

His retirement has left a void in world cuisine that may never be filled. It is some consolation to know that Switzerland now boasts more fine restaurants per square mile than any other country, thanks to the example set by Girardet, which many now seek to emulate.

His gift to us is this book of recipes, hand-picked from among the hundreds of creative dishes that have been landmarks for his clientele throughout his years of culinary delight.

A Reader's Guide

As in Frédy Girardet's first book, most recipes are divided into different stages:

Preparation includes every step that can be completed in advance—for example, in the morning for the evening. This is how things are done in professional kitchens, ensuring that a customer can be served whatever dish he has ordered within 15 minutes. By preparing the recipe in this way at home, you can avoid any last-minute panic.

Finishing Touches outlines those steps that must be completed only at the last moment. They rarely take more than 10 minutes.

When a recipe demands a longer cooking time, this section is entitled **Finishing Touches and Cooking.**

The **Presentation** section is for guidance. Be inspired to use your own imagination, but remember that food should be as seductive to the eye as to the palate.

The Golden Rules

Whether a dish is intended for a weekday meal or a festive occasion, it will only be successful if it is made with the best quality ingredients, cooked with precision, and properly seasoned.

The recipes in this book are suitable for everyday cooking if you follow these principles. Whether you wish to cook a fillet of fish, some poultry, a piece of meat, or a game bird, you will be sure to find a recipe that demonstrates the perfect technique and timing. And remember, you don't have to follow the recipes slavishly; they can always be simplified, except for a special occasion.

It Goes Without Saying

We have taken care to avoid using professional culinary terms in the recipes, and to repeat all useful instructions, but it goes without saying that vegetables must always be washed and peeled before cooking, so we have not specified this in the recipes.

In the Preparation section, however, we always specify when a cut or chopped ingredient should be placed in an airtight container and kept cool, and it is essential to follow these guidelines.

Over to You

You loved the first book, you successfully cooked a good number of the recipes it contained, but you have the impression that the recipes in this book are more difficult. You are both right and wrong.

Right, because since the first book was published, restaurant cooking has become more sophisticated, especially in terms of presentation. Wrong, because you can very easily simplify the various stages, by leaving out some or all of the purely decorative elements, which add a certain something to the finished dish, but are by no means indispensable.

Even if they are reduced to nothing more than the main element and the sauce, the recipes in this book will improve and enhance the culinary skills of most amateur cooks. Why not reap the benefit?

Frédy Girardet's logo since 1975, designed by Julien van der Wal, VDW Geneva.

Cold Appetizers

Aiguillettes of Goose Foie Gras with Walnuts, Raisins, and Vintage Madeira Gelée

Serves 4

³/₄ cup raisins
¹/₂ cup walnut halves
¹/₂ cup hazelnuts, skinned
2¹/₂ cups red wine gelée (page 199)
Salt and freshly ground pepper
Scant ¹/₂ cup white port
Scant ¹/₂ cup vintage Madeira
4 scallops of goose foie gras,
   3¹/₂ ounces each, ³/₄ inch thick
All-purpose flour, for dusting
1¹/₂ cups mesclun leaves
1 tablespoon wine vinegar
2 tablespoons peanut oil
1 tablespoon walnut oil
Guérande *fleur de sel*, for garnish
Cracked white peppercorns, for
   garnish
Sliced brioche or country bread,
   for serving

Preparation

1   Soak the raisins in lukewarm water overnight (or for at least 4 hours), then drain them.

2   Add the walnuts and hazelnuts to the raisins, and coarsely chop them all.

3   Combine this mixture with 2 cups of the wine gelée to make the stuffing for the scallops. Season with salt and pepper.

4   Combine the port and Madeira in a small saucepan and boil fiercely to reduce to a small spoonful of jam-like syrup. Heat the remaining ¹/₂ cup of wine gelée and mix it into the syrup to loosen it a little. Taste, and season with salt and pepper. Leave to cool slowly at room temperature.

5   Season the scallops with salt and pepper, and dust them lightly with flour. Heat a nonstick skillet until very hot and put in the scallops. Sear them for 40 seconds on each side. Pat them dry with paper towels, then cool quickly in the refrigerator.

6   When the scallops are cold, but still malleable, slit each one lengthwise through the middle, and fill with the stuffing mixture. Return them to the refrigerator for a few minutes.

7   As soon as the jelly mixture begins to set, brush it over the scallops to coat them. Repeat the operation several times until they are well coated, then return them to the refrigerator.

8   Wash the mesclun, spin it dry, and place in a plastic bag until ready to use.

9   Make a vinaigrette with the vinegar, oils, salt, and pepper.

Finishing Touches and Presentation

1   Toss the mesclun leaves in the vinaigrette.

2   Slice the stuffed scallops lengthwise about ¹/₄ inch thick, and fan the slices out attractively on each plate. Sprinkle with a little *fleur de sel* and cracked white peppercorns.

3   Garnish each one with a small mound of salad.

4   Serve with a slice of brioche or toasted country bread.

Lightly Jellied Chicken Bouillon with Truffled Foie Gras and Mousseline of Peas

Serves 4

2 sheets leaf gelatin
1½ ounces black truffle
3½ ounces terrine of foie gras
⅔ cup shelled peas (fresh or frozen)
Scant ½ cup whipping cream
Salt and freshly ground pepper
1¼ cups chicken stock (page 194)

Preparation

1 Soften the gelatin sheets in cold water.

2 Cut part of the truffle into 28 tiny (¹/₁₆-inch) dice, and chop the rest.

3 Press the foie gras terrine through a sieve to make a purée, and mix in the chopped truffle. Divide this mixture between the bottoms of four small (3-inch diameter) Asian-style bowls, and place in the refrigerator.

4 To make the pea mousseline, cook the peas in boiling salted water for 3 minutes, drain, and refresh in ice water. Drain, and spread on a cloth to dry thoroughly.

5 Put the cream in a saucepan, bring to a boil, then remove the pan from the heat. Squeeze one gelatin sheet between your hands to extract all the water, add it to the cream, and stir until completely melted. It may be necessary to return the pan to the heat for a moment. Add the peas to the hot cream, transfer to a blender, and purée. Season the purée with salt and pepper, then press through a fine sieve and let cool a little. Put the cooled purée on top of the foie gras in the bowls, and return to the refrigerator.

6 Pour the chicken stock into a small saucepan and reduce it by half over a high heat. Squeeze the second gelatin sheet to extract all the water, stir it into the stock until melted, and remove the pan from the heat.

7 Let stock cool until it has half-set to a light gelée, then stir in the diced truffle.

Finishing Touches and Presentation

1 If the truffled gelée has already set, warm it gently until half-set, and spoon it into the bowls.

2 Serve immediately, while the gelée is still trembling.

Cold Velouté of Trout in a Saffron Gelée with Osetra Caviar

Preparation

1 Peel and seed the cucumber. Cut the flesh into $1/8$-inch dice.

2 Bring a saucepan of water to a boil. Cut a cross in the tomatoes, plunge them into the boiling water for 15 seconds, then immediately plunge them into cold water, and skin and seed them. Cut the flesh of two of the tomatoes into $1/8$-inch dice. Coarsely chop the other two tomatoes.

3 Peel and finely chop the garlic and shallot.

4 To make the tomato coulis, heat the olive oil in a saucepan, add the garlic and shallot, and cook gently over a medium heat until the shallot is translucent. Add the chopped tomatoes and cook gently, stirring occasionally, until all the liquid has evaporated.

5 Meanwhile, finely snip the basil leaves.

6 When the tomato coulis is the right consistency, whizz it briefly with a hand blender, then add the basil. Season with salt and pepper and set aside.

7 Cut the trout fillets into $1/2$-inch dice. Season with cayenne pepper, salt, and pepper. Heat the butter in a skillet and cook the diced trout gently for 20 seconds. Drain, and reserve the cooking butter.

8 Finely snip enough dill to obtain 2 tablespoons, mix half into the diced trout, and reserve the rest.

9 To make the trout velouté, put $3/8$ cup of the fish gelée in a saucepan, and reduce by half over medium-high heat. Add the reserved trout-cooking butter.

10 Put the cream in a saucepan and reduce it by one-third. Add the reduced fish gelée, adjust the seasoning, strain through a fine sieve, cover, and set aside.

11 To make the saffron gelée, bring the remaining fish gelée to a boil, add the saffron, and simmer very gently for 2 minutes. Season with salt and pepper, strain through a fine sieve, and set aside.

Finishing Touches

1 Carefully mix the diced trout with $3/4$ ounce of the caviar, $1/2$ cup of the diced tomatoes, and $1/4$ cup of the diced cucumber.

2 Divide this mixture between four small (3-inch diameter) Asian-style bowls. Cover with $1/4$-inch layer of saffron gelée (if necessary, reheat to liquefy it a little), and place the bowls in the refrigerator to set the gelée.

3 Add a $1/2$-inch layer of trout velouté to the bowls and return to the refrigerator until set.

4 Divide the tomato coulis between the bowls and finish with a thin layer of saffron gelée. Return to the refrigerator until set.

5 Pour over the remaining trout velouté and refrigerate until set.

6 Mix together the remaining diced cucumber, diced tomato, and snipped dill, and divide this mixture between the bowls. Warm the remaining saffron gelée to liquefy it and pour a thin layer into each bowl. Refrigerate for at least 1 hour.

Serves 4

$1/4$ European cucumber
4 tomatoes
1 clove garlic
1 shallot
1 tablespoon olive oil
2 fresh basil leaves
Salt and freshly ground pepper
$3 1/2$ ounces trout fillets
Ground cayenne pepper
1 tablespoon unsalted butter
1 small bunch dill
$1 1/4$ cups fish gelée (page 199)
Scant $3/4$ cup whipping cream
Pinch of saffron powder
$2 1/4$ ounces osetra caviar

Presentation
Spoon a small quenelle of caviar into each bowl, decorate with a sprig of dill, and serve well chilled.

Chartreuse of Foie Gras with a Clear Gelée of Vendange Tardive Wine

Serves 4

¹/₄ cup *vendange tardive* (late harvest) Pinot Gris

1¹/₄ cups clear gelée (page 198)

Salt and freshly ground pepper

2¹/₂ cups broccoli florets

¹/₂ cup pistachio nuts, shelled

10 ounces terrine of foie gras

³/₄ ounce black truffle

1 tablespoon fresh Italian parsley leaves

1 cup mesclun leaves

1 tablespoon wine vinegar

2 tablespoons peanut oil

³/₄ cup chicken consommé (page 195)

Preparation

1 Put the Pinot Gris in a saucepan and reduce by half. Add the clear gelée, mix, take the pan off the heat, and season with salt and pepper.

2 To make the filling, cook the broccoli for 3 minutes in boiling salted water. Drain, refresh in ice water, and drain thoroughly. Finely chop the florets, add a few of the pistachio nuts and just enough Pinot Gris gelée to bind the mixture.

3 Line four small (3-inch diameter) Asian-style bowls with plastic wrap taking care to smooth out any air bubbles.

4 Press the foie gras terrine through a sieve to make a purée.

5 Spread a thin layer of foie gras over the inside of each bowl. Cover this with a ¹/₂-inch layer of broccoli filling, and spread with another thin layer of foie gras.

6 Fill up the bowls with the remaining broccoli filling.

7 Spread a layer of foie gras over the top, smooth the surface, place in the refrigerator, and set overnight.

8 Finely chop the remaining pistachio nuts.

9 Chop the truffle, place in a bowl, and refrigerate.

10 Finely chop the parsley and keep in a cool, draft-free place.

11 Wash the mesclun leaves and spin dry. Place in a plastic bag and keep cool. Make a vinaigrette with the vinegar, oil, and salt and pepper.

Finishing Touches

1 Reheat a little of the Pinot Gris gelée until half-set, then stir in half the chopped pistachios.

2 Unmold the chartreuses onto a wire rack and brush them with gelée. Repeat several times until they are beautifully glazed.

3 Pour the chicken consommé into a small saucepan, add the chopped truffle, and heat until the consommé just begins to bubble. Immediately take the pan off the heat, and stir in the remaining pistachio gelée. Quickly pour it into a bowl, add the parsley and the remaining pistachios, season with salt and pepper, and chill over ice or in the refrigerator.

4 Dress the mesclun leaves with the vinaigrette.

Presentation

Coat the bottom of 4 plates with a thin layer of the slightly cooled truffle, pistachio, and parsley consommé.

Arrange a chartreuse on each plate, and cut it into slices like a cake. Slightly pull out one slice as if to serve it.

Decorate with a small mound of dressed mesclun.

Chaud-Froid of Langoustines with Asian Spices and Apples

Serves 4

12 very large langoustines
1 tablespoon curry powder
1 tablespoon all-purpose flour
1 egg yolk, lightly beaten
³/₄ ounces sesame seeds

American Sauce
Claws and shells from the langoustines
2 shallots
1 small carrot
¹/₂ celery stalk
2 tablespoons olive oil
1 tablespoon tomato paste
1 tablespoon peeled, seeded, and
  chopped tomato
1 small clove garlic
1 tablespoon finely chopped fresh
  tarragon
¹/₄ cup white port
Scant ³/₄ cup water
¹/₄ cup white wine
Dash of Cognac
2 teaspoons unsalted butter, melted

Curry Mayonnaise
1 egg yolk
1 level tablespoon Dijon mustard
Salt and freshly ground pepper
Scant ³/₄ cup curry oil (page 199)
¹/₂ to 1 tablespoon white wine vinegar

1 small Granny Smith apple
1 tablespoon fresh lemon juice
1 cup mesclun leaves
¹/₂ cup Italian parsley
¹/₂ cup fresh dill
1 tablespoon wine vinegar
2 tablespoons olive oil
Salt and freshly ground pepper
1 tablespoon clarified butter

Preparation

1 Shell the langoustines, leaving on the last two tail sections of shell. Reserve the shells and claws for the sauce. Make a light incision all along their backs, and pull out the black intestinal thread. Season the langoustines with the curry, and very lightly dust only the backs with flour. Place on a plate, brush the backs with egg yolk, and sprinkle with sesame seeds. Cover with plastic wrap and refrigerate.

2 To make the sauce, chop the langoustine shells and claws. Peel and cut the shallots, carrot, and celery into ¹/₄-inch dice. Heat the oil in a saucepan until very hot, add the chopped shells and claws, and cook for 3 to 4 minutes. Add the tomato paste, stirring vigorously, then add the diced vegetables, chopped tomato, garlic, and tarragon. Cook for 2 minutes, stirring continuously, then moisten with the port, water, wine, and Cognac. Cook gently for 20 minutes, then press the sauce through a fine sieve into another saucepan, and reduce to a scant ³/₄ cup. Remove from the heat, whisk in the butter, season, and cool.

3 To make the mayonnaise, combine the egg yolk, mustard, and a little salt and pepper in a bowl, and gradually add the curry oil in a thin, steady stream, whisking continuously until thick. Thin the mayonnaise with some or all of the vinegar; it should be very fluid.

4 Peel and core the apple, and cut the flesh into ¹/₈ by ¹/₄-inch batons. Place in a small bowl, sprinkle with the lemon juice, and set aside.

5 Wash the mesclun leaves, parsley, and dill and spin them dry. Discard any large parsley and dill stalks. Reserve a few sprigs of dill for the garnish, then mix the rest with the mesclun. Place in a plastic bag and keep cool.

6 Make a vinaigrette with the vinegar, olive oil, and salt and pepper.

Finishing Touches

1 Heat the clarified butter in a nonstick skillet. Season the langoustines with salt and pepper. Put them in the skillet on their backs, and sauté for 40 seconds, then turn them, and fry for 10 seconds on each side. Immediately transfer to a plate, so that they do not continue to cook.

2 Dress the salad with the vinaigrette.

Presentation
Spoon little puddles of curry mayonnaise around the plates. Using a small spoon, drizzle a ribbon of sauce over the top. Arrange three langoustines in a W on each plate, with the tails outward, and sprinkle diced apple along their backs.
Place a mound of salad at the point of the W, and garnish with sprigs of dill.

Scallop and Cockle Salad with Sherry Vinegar Dressing

Serves 4

12 large fresh scallops, preferably
    dry-pack or diver, shelled, washed,
    and trimmed

1 pound fresh cockles in the shell

1$\frac{1}{2}$ tablespoons unsalted butter

$\frac{1}{2}$ red bell pepper

$\frac{1}{2}$ yellow bell pepper

2 baby leeks, the size of your pinkie

7 ounces mesclun leaves

1 tablespoon mustard

2 tablespoons sherry vinegar

1 tablespoon soy sauce

5 tablespoons olive oil

Salt and freshly ground pepper

$\frac{1}{4}$ cup fresh chives

Grapeseed oil, for frying

Kosher salt, for serving

Fresh herbs, for garnish

Preparation

1 If the scallops are in the shell, remove them, wash in abundant cold water, and trim off the white side muscle. Place on a plate, cover with plastic wrap, and refrigerate.

2 Wash the cockles in several changes of water, as they are always full of sand. Place in a large saucepan with the butter, cover, and cook over high heat for 1 to 2 minutes, shaking the pan several times, until the cockles have opened. Drain and reserve the cooking juices. Strain the juices into a small saucepan through a fine sieve lined with damp muslin or doubled cheesecloth.

3 Shell the cockles, and put them into the strained cooking juice.

4 Remove the seeds and white ribs from the peppers, and cut the peppers into tiny dice. Cover and keep in a cool place.

5 Wash and trim the leeks, and cook them in boiling salted water for 3 to 4 minutes; they should still be crisp to the bite. Refresh in cold water, drain, and cut them on the diagonal into $\frac{1}{2}$-inch lengths. Place in an airtight container.

6 Wash the mesclun leaves and spin dry. Place in a plastic bag and keep cool.

7 In a salad bowl, make a vinaigrette with the mustard, sherry vinegar, soy sauce, olive oil, and salt and pepper.

8 Very finely snip the chives, and stir them into the vinaigrette.

Finishing Touches

1 Take the cockles out of their juice, and add them to the vinaigrette. Toss the mesclun and diced peppers in the vinaigrette.

2 Divide the mesclun between the middles of four large plates.

3 Arrange the leeks in a star shape around the edges of the plates, and place the cockles between them.

4 Pour a little grapeseed oil into a nonstick skillet, and heat until searingly hot. Season the scallops and cook them for 30 to 40 seconds on each side, depending on their thickness.

Presentation
Arrange 3 scallops on each pile of mesclun and season each with a few drops of vinaigrette, a little kosher salt, and a couple of grindings of pepper. Decorate the plates with a few sprigs of fresh herbs and shells, if you wish.

Galantine of Rabbit with Baby Vegetables

Serves 12

2 pounds plump rabbit legs and
   shoulders
1¼ pounds calf's feet, cut into pieces
4 cups white wine
1 cup carrot, peeled and cut
   into ¼-inch dice
1 cup onion, peeled and cut
   into ¼-inch dice
1 cup celery, cut into ¼-inch dice
1 cup leek, white part only, cut into
   ¼-inch dice
1 bouquet garni (fresh thyme, parsley,
   and bay leaf)
Salt and freshly ground pepper

Clarification

7 ounces lean ground beef
1 carrot, chopped
1 onion, coarsely chopped
White part of ½ leek, coarsely
   chopped
Sprig of tarragon, chopped
1 egg white

2 sheets leaf gelatin, softened in cold
   water (if needed)
7 ounces baby carrots
3½ ounces baby turnips
1 small bunch cilantro
1 small bunch curly parsley
1 small bundle of chives
2 large leeks
Unsalted butter, for greasing the
   terrine
9-ounce block of terrine of foie gras
1 tablespoon pink peppercorns
Dash of white wine vinegar

Presentation
Unmold the terrine and cut it into ½- to ¾-inch slices
with an electric carving knife. Serve the terrine on a
plate with a few seasonal salad leaves and, if you
wish, a coulis or cold sauce of your choice and slices
of toasted country bread.

Preparation and Cooking

1   Trim the rabbit pieces and using a pointed knife, remove all the membranes.

2   Plunge the pieces of calf's feet into a saucepan of cold water, bring to a boil, boil steadily for 3 minutes, then drain and refresh in cold water.

3   Put the pieces of rabbit and the calf's feet in a large saucepan, and pour in the wine and enough cold water to cover them generously.

4   Bring to a boil, skimming the surface. Add the diced vegetables and the bouquet garni, season with salt and pepper, and simmer gently until the rabbit is very tender and the flesh comes away easily from the bones.

5   Lift out the rabbit pieces with a slotted spoon, and continue to cook the pieces of calf's feet; since they will make the gelée, they need to cook for a total of 4 hours.

6   Take the rabbit off the bones, cut the flesh into pieces, and remove the sinews and fat.

7   After the calf's feet have been cooked for 4 hours, strain the cooking bouillon through a fine sieve, and return the bouillon to the saucepan. Cool completely.

8   When it is cool, make the clarification. Mix the ground beef, chopped vegetables, and tarragon with the egg white.

9   Add the clarification to the cold bouillon and bring it slowly to a boil. Once boiling, turn the heat down to very low, and simmer gently for 20 minutes, basting the clarification with the bouillon from time to time.

10   Very gently pour the bouillon through a fine sieve lined with damp muslin or doubled cheesecloth.

11   To check the consistency of the gelée, pour a tablespoonful onto a small plate and place in the freezer for 2 minutes. If it has set after this time, the gelée is ready. If not, bring it back to boil, and stir in 1 or 2 soaked gelatin leaves, squeezed completely dry, then remove from the heat. Taste for seasoning.

12   Peel the baby carrots and turnips and cook separately in boiling salted water. When they are tender, drain and cut into ¼-inch dice.

13   Wash, spin dry, and chop the cilantro and parsley, separately, and snip the chives.

14   Remove and discard the two outer leek leaves. Pull away the other leaves, one by one, and wash them thoroughly. Blanch for 3 minutes in boiling salted water, refresh in cold water, and drain. Spread the leaves out flat on a kitchen towel, cover with another towel, and press your hand down on the leaves to dry and keep them flat.

15   To assemble the dish, you will need a 12 by 3-inch terrine and a board that fits snugly just inside the top rim. Butter the inside of the terrine and line it with plastic wrap, taking care to eliminate any air bubbles. Line the inside with leek leaves, laying them so that they overlap slightly and hang over the sides of the terrine. Keep in a cool place.

16   Cut the foie gras into large dice and mix with the rabbit, diced carrots and turnips, chopped parsley, and the pink peppercorns. Season with salt and pepper, and add a dash of vinegar to taste.

17   If the gelée has already set, heat it to liquefy a little, then brush a layer of gelée all over the leeks inside the terrine. Before the gelée sets completely, sprinkle the cilantro and chives over the base. Fill the terrine with the mixture of rabbit, foie gras, and vegetables, and pour over the half-set gelée, tapping the terrine on the work surface to ensure that the gelée fills all the gaps. Fold the overhanging leek leaves over the top, place the board on top, and refrigerate the terrine for 12 hours.

Duck Terrine with Pistachios

Serves 12

Forcemeat

1 pound skinless, boneless duck meat

1 pound pork neck

7 ounces chicken livers

4 shallots

1 apple

6 slices white bread, without crust

⅝ cup whipping cream

2 tablespoons grapeseed oil

2 tablespoons salt, plus more for
  seasoning

½ teaspoon freshly ground pepper,
  plus more for seasoning

½ teaspoon four-spice powder
  (ground cloves, ginger, nutmeg,
  and white pepper)

¼ cup Cognac

Garnish

4 ounces chicken livers

4 ounces terrine of foie gras

4 ounces skinless, boneless duck meat

1 tablespoon grapeseed oil

1 tablespoon Cognac

½ cup pistachio nuts, shelled

9 ounces pure pork fat, finely sliced

1 sprig of thyme

2 bay leaves

Preparation

1 To make the forcemeat, cut the duck meat, pork, and chicken livers into
  1-inch cubes.

2 Peel and finely slice the shallots.

3 Peel, quarter, and core the apple, and finely slice it.

4 Soak the bread in the cream.

5 Heat the grapeseed oil in a large skillet, add all the cubed meats, and season with
  the salt, pepper, and four-spice powder. Sear over high heat for about 1 minute,
  stirring, then scoop everything into a large bowl. Add the cream-soaked bread
  and the Cognac, and stir to mix.

6 Put the shallots and apples in the same skillet, and cook over very low heat until
  soft. Mix them into the forcemeat, and refrigerate until completely cold.

7 Pass the forcemeat through the coarse blade of a grinder, or chop coarsely in a
  food processor. Taste for seasoning.

8 To make the garnish, cut the chicken livers, foie gras, and duck meat into
  ½-inch dice.

9 Heat the oil in a skillet until very hot, add the diced chicken livers and duck
  meat, sear for about 2 minutes, and season. Transfer to a bowl and cool before
  adding the foie gras, Cognac, and pistachio nuts.

Finishing Touches and Cooking

1 You will need a 12 by 3-inch ovenproof terrine with a lid, a board that will fit
  just inside the rim covered with plastic wrap, and a 2-pound weight. Preheat the
  oven to 300°F and put in a bain-marie, half-filled with water to heat.

2 Mix the garnish with the forcemeat.

3 Line the terrine with the pork fat, reserving one slice. Fill the terrine with the
  forcemeat mixture, packing it down firmly. Cover the top with the reserved slice
  of fat, place the thyme and bay leaves on top, and put on the lid.

4 Place the terrine in the hot bain-marie, and cook for 1 to 1½ hours, until a meat
  thermometer inserted into the center indicates that the internal temperature has
  reached 150°F.

5 Take the terrine out of the bain-marie, and place in a roasting pan or deep dish.
  Cool it rapidly by trickling cold water into the pan.

6 When the terrine is cold, remove the lid, place the board and weight on top, and
  refrigerate for 48 hours before serving.

Wild Boar Terrine with Horn-of-Plenty Mushrooms

Preparation

1 The night before you make the terrine, cut the wild boar tenderloin for the garnish into ⅝-inch dice. Season with salt, pepper, and ½ teaspoon of the four-spice powder. Cut the raw foie gras the same way, and mix with the tenderloin. Pour the port and the 2 tablespoons Cognac over the tenderloin and foie gras, stir, cover, and marinate overnight in the refrigerator.

2 The following day, soak the mushrooms in warm water.

3 To make the forcemeat, cut the wild boar, pork neck, and pork liver into 1¼-inch dice, and season with the salt, pepper, and the remaining ½ teaspoon four-spice powder. Heat the oil in a large skillet until very hot, add the meats, and sear quickly for 1 minute, stirring. Transfer the meats to a platter and let cool. Keep the oil and juices in the skillet.

4 Peel, core, and finely slice the apple; peel 2 of the shallots, and the garlic. Add 1 tablespoon of the butter to the skillet, return it to the heat, add the apple, shallots, and garlic, and sauté gently until soft. Remove from the skillet with a spatula and scatter over the cooked meat.

5 Place the skillet over high heat, and deglaze with the ¼ cup Cognac, scraping up all the juices. Pour over the meats.

6 Cut the duck foie gras into 1¼-inch dice, and add to the cooled meats.

7 Pass the mixture through the fine blade of a grater, or grind in a food processor.

8 Drain and dry the mushrooms, clean them, and chop coarsely. Peel and finely chop the third shallot. Heat a small nonstick skillet until very hot, add the mushrooms, season with salt, and cook until the moisture has almost evaporated. Add the shallot and the remaining tablespoon of butter, stir for 2 minutes, then transfer to a plate, and let cool.

9 Add the mushrooms, cream, and egg to the forcemeat, and mix thoroughly.

Finishing Touches and Cooking

1 You will need a 12 by 3-inch ovenproof terrine with a lid, a board that will fit just inside the rim covered with plastic wrap, and a 2½-pound weight. Preheat the oven to 300°F, and put in a bain-marie half-filled with water.

2 Line the terrine evenly with the sliced pork fat, leaving the ends overhanging the edges.

3 Half-fill the terrine with forcemeat and press it down firmly with a small spatula.

4 Spread the ingredients for the garnish on top, then fill up the terrine with the remaining forcemeat.

5 Fold the overhanging pork fat over the surface, and place the thyme and bay leaves on top. Put on the lid, stand the terrine in the hot bain-marie, and cook in the oven for 1 to 1½ hours, until a meat thermometer inserted into the center indicates that the internal temperature has reached 150°F.

6 Remove the lid, and cool the terrine quickly by standing it in a deep dish and trickling in cold water. Place the board and weight on top, and refrigerate the terrine for 48 hours before serving.

Serves 12

5 ounces wild boar tenderloin
Salt and freshly ground pepper
1 teaspoon four-spice powder
 (ground cloves, ginger, nutmeg,
 and white pepper)
4½ ounces raw foie gras
2 tablespoons port
¼ cup plus 2 tablespoons Cognac
¾ ounce dried horn-of-plenty
 mushrooms

Forcemeat
1 pound wild boar meat
9 ounces pork neck
5 ounces pork or rabbit liver
1 ounce salt
½ teaspoon freshly ground pepper
2 tablespoons grapeseed oil
1 apple
3 shallots
1 clove garlic
2 tablespoons unsalted butter
5 ounces raw duck foie gras
Scant ¾ cup whipping cream
1 egg

9 ounces pure pork fat, finely sliced
1 thyme sprig
2 bay leaves

Breton Lobster with Asparagus Tips
and Vin Santo Vinaigrette

Serves 4

4 live lobsters, 1 pound 2 ounces each

32 small green asparagus spears

1 egg yolk

Scant ¹/₂ cup grapeseed oil

Juice of ¹/₂ lemon

Salt and freshly ground pepper

1 level tablespoon finely chopped
    fresh curly parsley

1 level tablespoon finely snipped
    fresh chervil

¹/₂ tablespoon strong mustard

2 tablespoons *agretto di vin santo* or
    best-quality white wine vinegar

4 to 5 tablespoons walnut oil

1 cup crisp baby lettuce

Preparation and Finishing Touches

1 Bring a large saucepan of salted water to a boil, and plunge in the lobsters. When the water comes back to a boil, cook the lobsters for 2 minutes, then drain. Leave them to cool, then detach the claws and legs. Remove the head shells, and take out the corals. Remove the claw meat. Discard the intestinal tract from the tails, and cut each tail into ten rings. Put all the meat on a plate and cover with plastic wrap.

2 Wash the asparagus carefully and cut the tips into 1¹/₂-inch lengths on the diagonal. Cook the tips only in boiling salted water for 2 to 3 minutes, until still slightly crunchy. Lift them out of the water, refresh in cold water, place on a plate, and cover with plastic wrap.

3 Cut the tender part of the asparagus stalks nearest the tips into 1¹/₂-inch lengths, and cook them in the minimum possible boiling salted water until very tender. Drain and refresh. Reserve the cooking water to thin the mayonnaise. Finely purée the cooked asparagus stalks in a food processor.

4 To make the green mayonnaise, put the egg yolk in a bowl, and gradually add the oil in a steady stream, whisking until thickened. Add 3 tablespoons of the asparagus purée and a little of the lemon juice. The mayonnaise should have a light coating consistency. If necessary, stir in 1 or 2 tablespoons of the asparagus-cooking water to thin it. Season with salt and pepper, and mix in the parsley and chervil.

5 Make a vinaigrette with the mustard, *agretto di vin santo,* walnut oil, and salt and pepper. Toss the rounds of lobster tail and claw meat, the asparagus tips, and the lettuce leaves in the vinaigrette.

Presentation

Pour a little green mayonnaise on to each plate, and spread it in a circular motion with the back of a soup spoon. Arrange 5 rounds of lobster tail and a piece of claw meat on top, and add a little mound of salad and a bouquet of 8 asparagus tips. If you wish, decorate each plate with a half lobster head.

Fine Velouté of Petits Pois with Frogs' Legs and Osetra Caviar

Serves 4

6 dozen frogs' legs

2 tablespoons unsalted butter

Salt and freshly ground pepper

1 shallot

$^1/_2$ cup sweet white wine

$^1/_2$ cup dry white wine

$^1/_4$ cup clear gelée (page 198)

$^5/_8$ cup whipping cream

$^1/_2$ cup extra-small frozen petits pois

2 ounces osetra caviar

12 small sprigs of chervil

Preparation

1   Bone out the frogs' legs by running a knife along both sides of the bones and removing them. Keep the meat from the thighs and the lower leg separate, and reserve the bones. Heat 1 tablespoon of the butter in a skillet, and cook the thigh meat for 1 minute. Season and put in a bowl. Repeat with the lower leg meat, and put in a separate bowl.

2   To make the frogs' leg gelée, peel and finely chop the shallot, put it in the skillet with the bones, and cook gently in the remaining tablespoon of butter. Add $^3/_4$ cup water and the two wines, and bring to a boil, skimming the surface. Decrease the heat and simmer gently for 20 minutes.

3   Add one-third of the clear gelée, season, and strain through a fine sieve lined with damp muslin or doubled cheesecloth. Cool quickly over ice.

4   To make the velouté, pour the cream into a saucepan, add the petits pois, and boil for 3 minutes. Add another third of the clear gelée, purée in a blender, then strain the velouté through a fine sieve, and cool over ice.

Finishing Touches

1   Divide the thigh meat between 4 small (3-inch diameter) Asian-style bowls.

2   Slightly warm the frogs' leg gelée, mix in $^3/_4$ ounce of the caviar, spoon this over the thigh meat, and refrigerate until set.

3   Cover the gelée with the velouté, and refrigerate until set.

4   Warm the remaining clear gelée. Garnish the bowls with the lower leg meat, cover with a thin layer of gelée, and refrigerate again until set.

Presentation
Decorate each bowl with 3 chervil sprigs. Shape the remaining caviar into 12 mini-quenelles, using two coffee spoons, and arrange three quenelles in a star shape on top of each bowl. Serve chilled.

Frivolity of Langoustines with Baby Leeks

Preparation

1 Pull off the langoustine tails and peel off the shells, leaving on the last two rings. Remove and discard the black intestinal thread, place the tails on a plate, cover with plastic wrap, and refrigerate.

2 Discard the outer leaves and half the green parts of the leeks. Cut the rest of the green parts into very small dice.

3 Blanch the white parts of the leeks in boiling salted water for 3 to 5 minutes, until tender, refresh in cold water, drain, and cut on the diagonal into ³/₄-inch lengths. Set aside.

4 In a small skillet, heat 1 tablespoon of the olive oil with the saffron. Add the cauliflower florets and cook gently for 2 minutes. Deglaze with 2 tablespoons of the vinegar and 2 tablespoons water, season with salt, and cook for a few more minutes, taking care to keep the cauliflower still slightly crunchy. Remove with a slotted spoon and set aside.

5 Cut open the chile and carefully scrape out all the seeds. Chop very finely.

6 Put the egg yolk in a bowl with the mustard and a little salt and pepper, and make a mayonnaise by whisking in 3 tablespoons of the olive oil and the sunflower oil. Thin the mayonnaise with 1 tablespoon of the vinegar, then stir in the diced leek greens and all or part of the chopped chile according to taste.

7 Make a vinaigrette with the remaining 1 tablespoon vinegar, 2 tablespoons of the olive oil, salt, and pepper.

Finishing Touches

1 Toss the leek whites in the vinaigrette.

2 Mix the whipped cream into the mayonnaise to lighten it. Taste and adjust the seasoning with a few drops of lemon juice, if necessary.

3 Season the langoustines. Heat the remaining 1 tablespoon olive oil in a skillet until very hot, put in the langoustines, and cook for no longer than 20 seconds on each side. Drain on paper towels.

Serves 4

12 large langoustines
4 baby leeks
7 tablespoons olive oil
Pinch of ground saffron
24 cauliflower florets
4 tablespoons white wine vinegar
Salt
1 small bird's eye or serrano chile
  (optional)
1 egg yolk
1 tablespoon strong mustard
Freshly ground pepper
3 tablespoons sunflower oil
1 tablespoon whipped cream
1 to 2 teaspoons fresh lemon juice
Chervil sprigs, for garnish

Presentation
Spoon a circle of mayonnaise in the center of each plate (you will have some left over, but it is difficult to make a smaller quantity!). Arrange 3 langoustines in a star shape on top, with the tails facing outward. Surround the langoustines with the leek whites, alternating with the cauliflower florets. Garnish with a few sprigs of chervil.

Hot Appetizers

Scallops of Duck Foie Gras with Green Lentils, Celeriac Fondant, and Hazelnut Vinaigrette

Serves 4

1 cup Puy lentils

1 pound 2 ounces celeriac
  (celery root)

Salt

Juice of 1 lemon

1 orange

$\frac{1}{4}$ cup sugar

$\frac{1}{4}$ cup *agretto di vin santo* or best-
  quality white wine vinegar

$\frac{1}{2}$ cup hazelnut oil

Freshly ground pepper

3$\frac{1}{2}$ ounces cooked beet

1 cup mixed fresh herbs, such as
  watercress, tarragon, Italian parsley,
  chives, or dill

4 sprigs chervil

All-purpose flour, for coating

4 scallops of duck foie gras,
  3$\frac{1}{2}$ ounces each, about 1-inch thick

2 tablespoons unsalted butter

Preparation

1 Cook the lentils as directed in the recipe on page 57, halving the quantities. Meanwhile, peel the celeriac, and slice it into 1 by $\frac{1}{4}$-inch thick triangles. Bring a saucepan of water to a boil, add salt, the lemon juice, and the celeriac, and cook until tender.

2 Scrub the orange under hot water and dry it. Peel off the zest with a swivel peeler, taking care not to remove any of the white pith. Cut 1 tablespoon of the zest into very fine 2-inch-long julienne. Put these in a colander, and plunge into boiling water for 30 seconds, then drain.

3 In a small saucepan, make a syrup with the sugar and $\frac{1}{4}$ cup water. Bring to a boil, toss in the orange julienne, simmer for 3 minutes, drain, and set aside.

4 Make a vinaigrette with the *agretto di vin santo,* hazelnut oil, salt, and pepper.

5 Peel the beet if necessary, and cut into $\frac{1}{4}$- by 1-inch-long batons. Place in a small bowl, and toss with a little of the vinaigrette.

6 Pick off the leaves of the mixed herbs, wash, dry in a salad spinner, and place in a plastic bag to keep fresh. Pick off the chervil leaves, and place in another plastic bag.

Finishing Touches

1 Drain the lentils and toss them in a little of the vinaigrette. Divide between the middle of 4 plates.

2 Season and lightly flour the foie gras scallops.

3 Heat a dry nonstick skillet until very hot, put in the foie gras, and sear for 40 seconds on each side. Drain on paper towels.

4 At the same time, heat the butter in a skillet, add the celeriac triangles, and cook until just golden. Season with salt and pepper.

5 Toss the herb mixture in the remaining vinaigrette.

Presentation
Place the foie gras on the lentil salad, and arrange
3 celeriac triangles on each escalope. Arrange
the beet batons around the edges, like the spokes
of a wheel. Put a small bouquet of dressed herbs on
one side, and garnish with the orange julienne and
chervil leaves.

Rabbit Béatilles with Asparagus Risotto

Serves 4

12 thin green asparagus spears
11 ounces rabbit livers
6 rabbit kidneys
Sprig Italian parsley
Sprig chervil

Risotto

1/4 cup unsalted butter, plus
   1 tablespoon
1 onion, chopped
1 cup arborio rice
About 3 cups hot chicken stock
   (page 194)
Scant 3/4 cup whipping cream
1/2 cup freshly grated Parmigiano-
   Reggiano
Salt and freshly ground pepper

1 tablespoon grapeseed oil
1 shallot, peeled and chopped
1 tablespoon white wine
3 small tablespoons brown veal stock
   (page 197)
1/4 cup shavings of Parmigiano-
   Reggiano

Preparation

1 Remove the bases of the asparagus, leaving the tips about 2 1/2 inches long, cook for 3 to 4 minutes in boiling salted water, refresh in cold water, and drain.

2 Dice the rabbit livers. Peel off the membrane from the kidneys, and cut them in half. Place the meats on a plate, cover with plastic wrap, and refrigerate.

3 Pick off the parsley and chervil leaves, and reserve them in an airtight plastic bag.

Finishing Touches and Cooking

1 To make the risotto, melt the 1/4 cup butter in a saucepan, add the onion, and cook gently until translucent. Add the rice and stir for a few minutes until the grains are almost completely transparent. Pour in enough of the chicken stock to cover the rice, and continue to cook, stirring continuously. When all of the stock has been absorbed, continue adding a little more, as soon as it is gone. After about 15 minutes, taste a grain of rice to test if it is cooked; it should still be slightly al dente. Keep stirring and tasting until the rice is perfect.

2 Add just enough cream and Parmigiano-Reggiano as needed to obtain a perfect, creamy consistency; stir, taste, and season with salt and pepper.

3 Just before the risotto is ready, reheat the asparagus tips in the remaining tablespoon of butter.

4 Heat the grapeseed oil in a skillet, add in the rabbit livers and kidneys, season, and sauté quickly for 30 seconds. Add the shallot and cook for another 30 seconds, then scoop out onto a plate, and keep the skillet to make the jus.

5 Discard the fat from the skillet, deglaze with 2 tablespoons water, the wine, and the veal stock, and simmer for a few minutes. Season, and remove from the heat.

Presentation
Divide the risotto between the centers of 4 plates, and mound the livers and kidneys on top. Garnish each one with 3 asparagus tips, a few shavings of Parmigiano-Reggiano, and a few parsley and chervil leaves. Sprinkle a few drops of jus over the livers and kidneys, and serve the rest of the jus on the side.

Warm Native Oysters in Champagne with Green Onion and Bell Pepper Compote and Caviar

Preparation

1 Peel the green onions, and cut them on the diagonal into ¹/₂-inch lengths.

2 Peel the bell peppers with a swivel peeler, open them up, and remove all the seeds and white ribs. Cut the flesh ¹/₂ inch thick, lengthwise, and discard any parts that do not lie flat. Cut the lengths into ¹/₂-inch lozenge shapes. Blanch the two different-colored peppers separately in boiling salted water for 1 minute each, then drain.

3 Open the oysters over a bowl to catch the juices, and strain the juices into a small saucepan. Reserve the oysters. Add the champagne and reduce over medium-high heat to about 4 tablespoons.

Finishing Touches

1 To make the green onion and bell pepper compote, gently cook the onions in 1 tablespoon of the butter until softened, moisten with 1 tablespoon water, and cook for another minute. Add the yellow and red bell pepper lozenges, and season.

2 Reheat the champagne reduction until it comes to a boil, take the pan off the heat, and drop in the oysters for 30 seconds, until just warm. Remove them with a slotted spoon. Cut the remaining butter into small pieces.

3 Stir the cream into the reduction, bring it just to a simmer, and thicken the sauce over very low heat by whisking in the butter pieces a little at a time, with a small whisk. Season with salt, pepper, and cayenne.

Serves 4

2 green onions, root ends trimmed
1 small yellow bell pepper
1 small red bell pepper
12 very large oysters such as Belon
Scant ³/₄ cup champagne
¹/₃ cup unsalted butter
1 tablespoon whipping cream
Salt and freshly ground white pepper
Ground cayenne pepper
³/₄ ounce caviar
Fresh chervil leaves, for garnish

Presentation
Arrange the oysters on warmed plates, and place a little green onion and bell pepper compote between each one. Coat the oysters with the sauce and put a few grains of caviar on top of each one. Garnish with the chervil leaves.

Steamed Bouchot Mussels with Clam Brochettes, White Wine, and Green Onions

Serves 4

12 green onions, root ends trimmed
9 ounces small mussels
10 ounces hard-shell clams
2 shallots
1 cup loosely packed Italian parsley
2 sprigs chervil

Clam Brochettes
32 hard-shell clams, shelled
1 egg yolk, lightly beaten
½ cup sesame seeds

Scant ⅔ cup unsalted butter
2 sprigs thyme
Salt and freshly ground pepper
Scant ¾ cup white wine
1 tablespoon clarified butter

Preparation

1 Peel the green onions and slice them thinly, including the green parts.
2 Scrub the mussels and clams under cold water, wash quickly in several changes of water, and drain.
3 Peel and finely chop the shallots, and keep in an airtight container in a cool place.
4 Wash, spin dry, and chop the parsley, pick off the chervil leaves, and keep them in separate airtight containers in a cool place.
5 To make the clam brochettes, season the shelled clams, and roll them first in the egg yolk, then in the sesame seeds to coat thoroughly. Skewer four clams on each of four toothpicks, place on a plate, cover with plastic wrap, and refrigerate.

Finishing Touches

1 Put the shallots in a large saucepan with 2 tablespoons of the butter, and cook over medium heat until translucent. Increase the heat to very high, add the mussels and thyme, pour in half of the wine, season with a few grindings of pepper, and cover the pan. Cook for 2 to 3 minutes, shaking the pan once or twice, or until the mussels have opened. Drain, straining the juices into a small saucepan.
2 Open the clams in the same way, using the rest of the wine. Drain, straining the juices into the pan with the mussel juices. Cut the remaining butter into small pieces.
3 Over high heat, reduce the shellfish juices to a scant ¾ cup, then decrease the heat to very low and thicken by whisking in the remaining butter a little at a time, with a small whisk. Remove the pan from the heat as soon as the butter has all been absorbed. Adjust the seasoning and add the sliced green onions.
4 Remove the top of the mussel shells, leaving the mussels on the half-shell. Leave the clams open, but still in their shells.
5 Heat the clarified butter in a skillet, and cook the clam brochettes for about 1½ minutes, turning them until golden all over.

Presentation
Divide the mussels between 4 large, warmed bowls, and arrange the clams on top. Pour the buttery juices over the mussels and clams, sprinkle with chopped parsley, and garnish each plate with 2 clam brochettes and some chervil leaves. Serve immediately.

Foie Gras à la Boulangère with Horseradish

3¹/₂ ounces fresh horseradish root

Scant ³/₄ cup chicken stock
   (page 194)

Scant ³/₄ cup brown veal stock
   (page 197)

¹/₄ cup sherry vinegar

Salt and freshly ground pepper

1 green onion, root end trimmed

14 ounces small, oval new potatoes

3 tablespoons clarified butter

4 scallops of duck foie gras,
   3¹/₂ ounces each, ³/₄-inch thick

All-purpose flour, for coating

Preparation

1 Peel the horseradish root. Cut approximately half of the root into 10 long, thin strips, then halve these lengthwise into very thin julienne. Place in an airtight container and keep cool.

2 To make the jus, grate the rest of the horseradish, place in a saucepan with the chicken stock, veal stock, and 2 tablespoons water, and cook for 5 minutes. Strain through a fine sieve into a small saucepan, pressing the horseradish to extract as much juice as possible. Add the vinegar and reduce the jus to about 3 tablespoons. Season with salt and pepper and set aside.

3 Halve the green onion lengthwise. Slice the white part into very thin semicircles, place in an airtight container, and keep cool. Finely snip the green tops, and reserve them in the same way.

4 Peel the potatoes and slice them very finely with a mandoline or the fine slicing blade of a food processor. If you are not going to cook them immediately, submerge them in cold water to prevent discoloration.

Finishing Touches

1 Lift the potatoes out of the water, using your hands so that the starch they exude is left in the water, and carefully sponge dry.

2 Heat 2 tablespoons of the clarified butter in a skillet over high heat, add the potatoes, and sauté until crispy and golden. Add the onion semicircles, stir gently for 1 minute, and season. Remove from the heat.

3 Season the foie gras scallops and lightly flour them. Heat a nonstick skillet until very hot, put in the scallops, and sear for 40 seconds on each side, then drain on paper towels.

4 At the same time, heat the remaining 1 tablespoon clarified butter until very hot, add the horseradish julienne, sauté for 1 minute, then remove with a slotted spoon.

5 Reheat the horseradish jus.

Presentation

Divide the potatoes between the centers of 4 warmed plates, and place a scallop on top. Pour a few drops of horseradish jus over the foie gras, and scatter the green onion tops and horseradish julienne over the top.

Cream of Asparagus with Truffles and Crayfish Tails

Preparation

1 Bring a large saucepan of water to a boil, and drop in the crayfish. When the water comes back to a boil, cook for 30 seconds, and drain. Shell the tails and remove the black intestinal thread. Place the tails on a plate and cover with plastic wrap. (Freeze the shells, and keep until you have enough to make a crayfish bisque.)

2 Cut the asparagus tips down to 2 inches long, and cook them for 4 to 5 minutes in boiling salted water. Refresh in cold water so that they retain their vivid color, and drain.

3 Cut off and discard the woody ends of the asparagus stalks. Cut the rest of the stalks into ³/₄-inch lengths, and cook in boiling salted water until tender. Drain, reserving the cooking water.

4 To make the cream of asparagus, peel and very finely chop the shallot. Place in a saucepan with 1 teaspoon of the butter, and cook gently over medium heat until translucent. Add a scant ³/₄ cup of the reserved cooking water and the chicken stock. Bring to a simmer, then add the cream and the drained asparagus stalks. Remove from the heat and purée in a food processor or blender, then press through a fine sieve, and adjust the seasoning. Set aside.

5 Cut the truffle into very fine julienne, place in an airtight container, and keep cool.

6 Pick the leaves off the chervil, place in a plastic bag, and keep cool.

Finishing Touches

1 Reheat the cream of asparagus, and enrich it by whisking in 2 tablespoons of the butter.

2 Reheat the asparagus tips in 1 teaspoon of the butter.

3 Heat the remaining teaspoon of butter in a skillet, toss in the truffle julienne, and heat for 30 seconds. Add the crayfish tails, season with a tiny pinch of cayenne, salt, and pepper, stir, and remove from the heat as soon as the crayfish tails are hot.

Serves 4

28 live red-clawed crayfish
2¹/₄ pounds asparagus
1 shallot
3 tablespoons unsalted butter
Scant ³/₄ cup chicken stock (page 194)
1¹/₄ cups whipping cream
Salt and freshly ground pepper
1¹/₂ ounces black truffle
4 sprigs of chervil
Ground cayenne pepper

Presentation
Divide the cream of asparagus between 4 large, warmed bowls. Arrange 7 asparagus tips like the spokes of a wheel on the base of each one, and mound 7 crayfish tails in the center. Scatter the truffle julienne and a few chervil leaves over the top.

Note: This dish can also be made with large cooked shrimp.

Warm Poached Eggs with Truffle Purée and Asparagus Velouté

Serves 4

28 thin asparagus spears
1½ cups whipping cream
Salt and freshly ground pepper
1 small shallot
3 ounces black truffles
1 tablespoon unsalted butter
1 tablespoon port
1 tablespoon old Madeira
5 ounces terrine of duck foie gras
Scant ¾ cup white wine vinegar
4 large eggs, straight from the
   refrigerator

Preparation

1 Cut the asparagus tips down to ¾ inch long, place in a small saucepan, barely cover with lightly salted water, and boil for 3 minutes. Refresh in cold water and drain, reserving the cooking water. Set aside.

2 Cut off and discard the woody ends of the asparagus stalks. Cut the rest of the stalks into ¾-inch lengths. Place in a saucepan, add the reserved cooking water, and add enough cold water to cover ¾ inch above the asparagus. Cook until very tender and drain, reserving a scant ¾ cup of the cooking water.

3 To make the asparagus velouté, combine the reserved cooking water and 1¼ cups of the cream in a saucepan, bring to a simmer, and add the drained asparagus stalks. Purée in a blender or food processor, and press through a fine sieve. Season with salt and pepper, and set aside.

4 Peel the shallot and chop it very finely.

5 Using a truffle shaver, slice the truffles wafer-thin. Use a decorative pastry cutter to cut the slices into ¾-inch crescents, reserving the trimmings. Place the crescents in an airtight container, and keep cool.

6 To make the truffle purée, finely chop the truffle trimmings, and place in a small saucepan with the butter and shallot. Cook over medium heat until the shallot is translucent, moisten with the port and Madeira, and reduce by half. Stir in the remaining ¼ cup cream, and continue to reduce until the cream thickly coats the chopped truffle and shallot. Season and set aside.

7 Crush the foie gras to a purée with a fork, or rub it through a coarse sieve. Place in an airtight container and refrigerate.

Finishing Touches and Presentation

1 Reheat the asparagus velouté.

2 Place a plain 1½-inch pastry cutter in the center of a shallow bowl, and make a ¾-inch base of puréed foie gras inside it. Spread the truffle purée over the foie gras and remove the pastry cutter. Repeat with the other three bowls.

3 In a wide shallow saucepan or deep skillet, bring 5 cups water and the vinegar to a simmering point.

4 Break the chilled eggs into separate cups. Add them to the simmering water, one at a time, and poach for 3 minutes. Lift them out, quickly rinse in hot water to eliminate the vinegary taste, then drain on a paper towel, and trim the edges to give the eggs an attractive round shape.

5 Place the eggs on the bed of foie gras and truffle purée, and decorate the eggs with the truffle crescents.

6 Arrange seven asparagus tips around each one, like the spokes of a wheel.

7 Pour the hot asparagus velouté carefully around the egg assembly, and serve immediately.

Baby Squid Cannelloni with Artichokes, Asparagus, and Saffron Cream

Serves 4

Saffron Ravioli Dough

3 eggs

1 tablespoon olive oil

1½ cups bread flour

Pinch of salt

¼ teaspoon powdered saffron

1 pound 2 ounces baby squid or
   cuttlefish

Scant ¾ cup extra virgin olive oil

Salt and freshly ground pepper

1 zucchini, washed

1 large clove garlic

2 shallots

1 bunch fresh chives

⅜ cup fresh tarragon leaves

1 cup fresh curly parsley leaves

1 cup fresh Italian parsley leaves

6 small violet artichokes

Juice of 1 lemon

20 thin asparagus spears

Saffron Cream

2 tablespoons finely chopped shallot

Leaves from a 2-inch sprig thyme

1 tablespoon olive oil

Scant ¾ cup fish stock (page 198)

½ teaspoon powdered saffron

1¼ cups whipping cream

Ground cayenne pepper

Salt and freshly ground pepper

Lemon juice

Saffron threads

1 tablespoon grapeseed oil

2 tablespoons unsalted butter,
   softened

¾ cup Parmigiano-Reggiano

Preparation

1 To make the saffron ravioli dough, lightly beat the eggs with the oil. Fit an electric mixer with the dough hook, sift the flour into the bowl, add the salt, saffron, and egg mixture, and mix until the dough forms itself into a ball. Wrap in plastic wrap, and refrigerate for 2 hours.

2 To make the filling, clean the squid or cuttlefish tubes and heads. Pick out 3½ ounces of the smallest for the garnish, wrap them in plastic wrap, and refrigerate. Heat a little of the olive oil in a skillet, and quickly sauté the rest of the squid until they turn opaque. Season with salt and pepper, drain, chop coarsely, and set aside. Do not wash out the skillet.

3 Cut ⅛-inch strips from the outside of the zucchini, including the skin, and cut these into ⅛-inch dice. Place in an airtight container and keep cool. Chop the rest of the zucchini flesh, discarding the seeds if necessary.

4 To make the filling, peel and finely chop the garlic and shallots. Put them and the chopped zucchini in the skillet in which you cooked the squid, add a little oil if necessary, and brown quickly. Season and mix with the chopped squid.

5 Finely chop one-third of the herbs, add them to the chopped squid mixture, and chop the mixture again with a large knife to even out the filling. Adjust the seasoning. Reserve the remaining herbs for the jus.

6 Cut the artichoke stems to 1½ inches and cut off the top thirds of all the leaves. Peel the artichoke stems and base, turning them as you would an apple, and cutting the stem into a point. Cut each artichoke heart into 10 pieces, and drop the pieces into a bowl of water acidulated with the lemon juice.

7 Cut the asparagus tips down to 2 inches, and blanch them in boiling salted water for 3 to 4 minutes. Refresh in cold water, drain, and set aside.

8 To make the saffron cream, put the shallot and thyme leaves in a small saucepan, add the oil, and cook over medium heat until the shallot is translucent. Add the fish stock and the saffron, and reduce the liquid by half over high heat. Add the cream and reduce gently, stirring, until it is thick enough to coat the back of a wooden spoon. Strain the saffron cream through a fine sieve into another saucepan, season with cayenne, salt, pepper, and 2 drops of lemon juice, and add a few saffron threads. Set aside.

9 Roll out the ravioli dough through the finest setting of a pasta machine, and cut it into 4-inch squares.

10 Boil a pan of salted water with the grapeseed oil, add the pasta squares, and cook until still firm but not al dente. Refresh the pasta in cold water, and lay the squares flat on a cloth to drain.

11 To assemble the cannelloni, lay a piece of filling the size of your index finger on each pasta square, ¾ inch in from one edge. Roll the pasta tightly around the filling, like a cigar, cut each roll in half crosswise, and trim the ends diagonally. Make the rest of the cannelloni in the same way. Place the cannelloni on a buttered baking sheet and brush them with 1 tablespoon of the butter. Cover with a damp cloth.

12 To make the herb jus, coarsely chop the remaining herbs and place in a blender with 3 tablespoons water, and purée. Pass the purée through a fine sieve into a small saucepan, pressing hard to extract all the juice. Bring the jus to a boiling point, whisk in the remaining tablespoon butter, season, and remove from the heat.

13 Using a truffle shaver, shave the Parmigiano-Reggiano into thin curls, place in an airtight container, and keep cool.

Finishing Touches and Cooking

1 Preheat the oven to 425°F.

2 In a pan, heat a little olive oil until hot, add the artichoke hearts, and sauté until golden. Add the asparagus tips, stir until heated through, and season.

3 In another pan, heat a little more olive oil, add the diced zucchini, sauté until golden, and season.

4 Remove the cloth from the cannelloni and cover them with a sheet of parchment paper. Place the baking sheet in the hot oven and heat the cannelloni for 3 to 4 minutes, watching carefully to ensure that they do not dry out.

5 Heat a nonstick skillet until very hot, pour in some olive oil, add the small squid you reserved for the garnish, and quickly sear them. Season and drain on paper towels.

6 Warm the herb jus.

Presentation
Spoon 2 tablespoons of saffron cream and
1 tablespoon of herb jus attractively on to each plate.
Place the cannelloni in the center and surround them
with the artichokes and asparagus tips. Garnish with
curls of Parmigiano-Reggiano, and scatter the sautéed
squid and the zucchini dice around the edges of
the plate.

Cream of Broccoli Soup with Wild Mushrooms

Serves 4

2½ pounds broccoli

10 ounces wild mushrooms (cèpes, chanterelles, mousserons, etc; one single variety or a mixture)

3 cups chicken stock (page 194)

⅝ cup whipping cream

Salt and freshly ground pepper

1 shallot

1½ tablespoons unsalted butter

Preparation

1 Cut off the broccoli florets and use only these for the soup. Wash and drain them. To make a vivid green soup, cook the florets, uncovered, in a large amount of boiling salted water for 5 minutes, until very well cooked. Drain, refresh in cold water so that they keep their color, and drain thoroughly.

2 Cut off and discard the earthy ends of the mushroom stalks. If you are using cèpes, simply wipe the caps with a cloth; wash all the other mushrooms briefly under running water.

3 Cut large mushrooms into approximately ⅛-inch slices, medium-sized mushrooms into quarters, and leave small ones whole. Place in an airtight container and keep cool.

4 Bring the chicken stock to a boil, pour it over the broccoli, and purée in a blender or a food processor. Pour the purée into a saucepan, add the cream, and season with salt and pepper. Strain the cream of broccoli through a fine sieve, and return it to the saucepan.

5 Peel the shallot and chop it very finely. Place in an airtight container and keep cool.

Finishing Touches

1 Reheat the soup.

2 Heat a nonstick skillet until very hot, add the mushrooms, season with salt, and stir with a wooden spoon until the mushrooms have released all their moisture. When it has almost completely evaporated, stir in the butter and shallot. Cook for 2 minutes, stirring continuously, then scoop the mushrooms onto paper towels to drain.

Presentation
Pour the soup into warmed individual tureens or soup plates and pile a mound of hot mushrooms into the center.

Spinach and Herb Ravioli with Parsley Jus

Serves 4

14 ounces ravioli dough (page 202)

1 cup fresh chervil

3¹/₂ cups firmly packed fresh curly
  parsley

1 cup firmly packed fresh Italian
  parsley

4 cups loosely packed spinach,
  about 4 ounces

2 shallots

1 tablespoon extra virgin olive oil

Salt and freshly ground pepper

¹/₄ cup fromage frais or Quark cheese

All-purpose flour, for dusting the
  work surface

1 large egg yolk

Semolina, for sprinkling

1 cup vegetable bouillon (page 194)

Pinch of cornstarch

1 tablespoon grapeseed oil

1 tablespoon unsalted butter

Mixed fresh herbs, for garnish

Preparation

1 Prepare the ravioli dough, roll it into a ball, wrap in plastic wrap, and leave to rest in the refrigerator for 2 hours.

2 For the filling, carefully pick off the leaves from the chervil, both types of parsley, and the spinach.

3 Fill a large saucepan with salted water, bring to a boil, toss in the parsley (not the chervil), and bring back to a boil for 5 minutes. Drain, refresh in cold water, and drain again.

4 Blanch the spinach leaves in the same way for 2 minutes, refresh, and drain well.

5 Peel the shallots and chop them very finely.

6 Take the drained parsley leaves, squeeze them tightly between your hands to extract all the water, then set aside about ¹/₄ cup of the parsley to use for the jus.

7 Put the olive oil and chopped shallots in a deep skillet, and sauté over medium heat until the shallots become translucent. Add the cooked parsley (except the ¹/₄ cup you reserved for the jus) and the spinach, stirring with a fork to untangle the leaves. Add the raw chervil, season with salt and pepper, stir for 30 seconds, and scoop onto a chopping board. Roughly chop the mixture with a knife and leave it to cool.

8 Mix in the fromage frais and season. Divide the mixture into 28 walnut-sized balls.

9 Roll the ravioli dough through the thinnest setting of a pasta machine. Divide it into 2 equal sheets, and spread them out completely flat on a floured board.

10 In a cup, mix the egg yolk with 1 tablespoon cold water, and brush it over one of the 2 sheets of dough. Arrange the 28 balls of filling on this sheet, spacing them 1¹/₂ inches apart. Gently lay the second sheet of dough over the top, and press your fingertips around each ball of filling to seal the dough sheets firmly together. Cut out the ravioli with a round, fluted pastry cutter, and place them on a plate sprinkled with a thin layer of semolina. Cover with a cloth to prevent them from drying out.

11 To make the parsley jus, put the reserved parsley and the vegetable bouillon in a blender or food processor. Blend to a purée, then pass through a fine sieve into a small saucepan, pressing the parsley to extract all the juices. Heat the jus.

12 Mix the cornstarch with 1 tablespoon cold water to make a paste, pour it into the parsley jus, stir, and remove from the heat.

Cooking

1 Fill a saucepan with plenty of salted water and bring to a boil. Add the grapeseed oil and the ravioli, and poach for about 3 minutes. Immediately drain and place on a cloth.

Finishing Touches

1 Reheat the parsley jus and check the seasoning.

2 Heat the butter in a frying pan, add the ravioli, season, and stir them gently until very hot.

Presentation
Warm 4 small, deep plates. Coat the bottom of each with a little parsley jus, and arrange the ravioli in a rosette on top. Decorate each plate with a mini-bouquet of fresh herbs.

Scallops in the Shell with Cockle Jus and Caviar

Serves 4

8 ounces fresh cockles, in the shell

1 small onion

3 tablespoons unsalted butter

1 sprig thyme

1 bay leaf

Scant ¾ cup white wine

4 large scallops in the shells, or use
 dry-pack or diver scallops, and
 bought scallop shells

2 green onions

Salt and freshly ground pepper

Kosher salt, for serving

Handful of fresh seaweed, for serving
 (optional)

Ground cayenne pepper

¼ cup whipping cream

Dash of kirsch

Fresh lemon juice

¾ ounce osetra caviar

Preparation

1 Wash the cockles in several changes of water, as they always contain a lot of sand.

2 Peel and chop the onion, place in a saucepan with 2 teaspoons of the butter, and cook over medium heat until translucent. Add the thyme, bay leaf, and cockles. Pour in the wine, cover the pan, and cook for about 1 minute, until the cockles have opened. Drain, reserving the juices. Strain the juices through a fine sieve lined with damp muslin or doubled cheesecloth into a small saucepan. Set over high heat, reduce to one-third, and set aside.

3 Take the cockles out of the shells and put them in the reduced cooking juices.

4 Open the scallops, keeping the two shells joined at the hinge. Hold them under cold running water, and remove the beards. Carefully, so as not to separate the shells, take out the scallops, and clean them removing the white muscle from the side. Place on a plate, cover with plastic wrap, and refrigerate.

5 Trim the green onions and cut them on the diagonal into ½-inch lengths. Place in a small saucepan with 1 tablespoon of the butter, and cook over medium heat until very soft. Season with salt and pepper and set aside.

6 Make a mound of kosher salt on each plate, and decorate with seaweed, if you wish.

Finishing Touches and Presentation

1 In the bottom of a steamer, bring 5 cups of water to a boil.

2 Season the scallops with salt, cayenne, and ground pepper. Place them in the scallop shells, and cover with softened green onions. Arrange the shells in the top part of the steamer, put on the lid, and steam for 3 to 4 minutes. Place one scallop on each plate.

3 Take the cockles out of their cooking juice, and reheat the juice. Using a wooden spoon, stir in the cream, then the remaining butter, the kirsch, and a few drops of lemon juice. Adjust the seasoning, return the cockles to the sauce, and spoon it around the scallops. Spoon a small quenelle of caviar onto each scallop.

Sweetbread Fritters with
Celeriac Cream and Deep-Fried Herbs

Serves 4

1 plump veal sweetbread, about
     1½ pounds

13 ounces celeriac (celery root),
     peeled

3½ ounces potatoes, peeled

1¼ cups chicken stock (page 194)

Salt

1¼ cups plus 1 tablespoon
     whipping cream

Freshly ground pepper

¾ ounce black truffle

3 tablespoons unsalted butter

Scant 1 cup, loosely packed fresh
     Italian parsley

About 1¼ cups loosely packed fresh
     curly parsley

About ¾ cup loosely packed fresh
     tarragon

½ cup peanut oil, for deep-frying

All-purpose flour, for dusting

3 tablespoons clarified butter

Preparation

1   Clean the sweetbread by rinsing for 3 to 4 hours under very slowly running cold water to remove all traces of blood. Using a small, sharp knife, carefully peel off all the membrane, sinews, and cartilage. Cut the sweetbread into ¾-inch dice, place on a plate, cover with plastic wrap, and refrigerate.

2   To make the celeriac cream, cut three-quarters of the celeriac and all of the potatoes into ½-inch dice. Cook them in the chicken stock with a pinch of salt until very tender. Add the cream, bring up just to a simmer, then strain through a fine sieve without pressing. Season with salt and pepper and set aside.

3   Cut the remaining celeriac and the truffle into very tiny dice. Gently heat them separately in 2 teaspoons butter, drain on paper towels, and stir them into the cream of celeriac.

4   Cut off the thick lower stalks of the herbs, and place the tops in an airtight container in a cool place.

Finishing Touches

1   Reheat the celeriac cream.

2   In a saucepan or deep-fat fryer, heat the oil to 300°F. Deep-fry the herbs until crispy, and drain on paper towels.

3   Season the diced sweetbread with salt and pepper, moisten slightly with the 1 tablespoon cream, dust with 2 pinches of flour, and mix well to coat the sweetbreads in a thick paste.

4   Heat the clarified butter in a skillet until very hot, add the sweetbread fritters, and quickly color them all over. Add the remaining whole butter, and continue to cook until the fresh butter is foamy. Adjust the seasoning and drain the sweetbreads on paper towels.

Presentation
Divide the celeriac cream between 4 warmed shallow
bowls, put the sweetbread fritters in the middle, and
garnish with the fried herbs.

Shellfish Marinière with Chervil

Preparation

1 Separately scrub the three varieties of shellfish in several changes of water. Be especially careful with the cockles, which are always full of sand.

2 Open all three varieties separately in the classic way: for each of the different shellfish, soften 1 tablespoon shallot in 1 tablespoon butter, add one type of shellfish, a bouquet garni, and one-third of the wine to each pan; cover the pans and cook for about 2 minutes, shaking the pans two or three times. Drain the shellfish, and reserve all the cooking juices. Remove the top shells, leaving them on the half-shell.

3 Combine the cooking juices, and strain them through a fine sieve lined with damp muslin or doubled cheesecloth into a saucepan.

4 Reduce by half, over high heat.

5 Pick off the chervil leaves, place in an airtight container, and keep cool.

Finishing Touches

1 Reheat the reduced cooking juices, and thicken by whisking in the remaining butter. As soon as the butter has all been absorbed, remove the pan from the heat, taste, season generously with pepper and, if necessary, a little salt.

Serves 4

1 quart mussels
1 pound fresh cockles, in the shell
1 pound small clams
3 tablespoons chopped shallots
$\frac{1}{2}$ cup unsalted butter
3 bouquets garnis (fresh thyme, parsley, and bay leaf)
Scant $\frac{1}{2}$ cup white wine
3 sprigs chervil
Salt and freshly ground pepper

Presentation
Divide the different shellfish evenly between 4 warmed bowls, coat them with the hot butter sauce, and scatter the chervil leaves on top.

Perciatelli Timbales with Frogs' Legs and Morel Mushrooms

Serves 4

Chicken Forcemeat

6 ounces skinless chicken fillets, well chilled

2$^1/_2$ cups heavy cream, well chilled

1 large egg white

Salt and freshly ground pepper

7 ounces fresh morel mushrooms

$^1/_4$ cup unsalted butter

1 tablespoon Madeira

$^1/_4$ cup whipping cream

12 frogs' legs

4 sprigs Italian parsley

12 ounces perciatelli

40 medium asparagus spears

Scant $^1/_2$ cup loosely packed fresh chervil

Cream of Frogs' Legs

1 shallot

1 tablespoon unsalted butter

2 parsley stalks

Bones and trimmings of the frogs' legs

Scant $^3/_4$ cup chicken stock (page 194)

Scant $^3/_4$ cup whipping cream

Ground cayenne pepper

Salt and freshly ground pepper

Note: You will need four cylindrical molds, 2 inches in diameter, 1$^1/_2$ inches deep, and four bands of thick aluminum foil, 10 by 1$^1/_2$ inches.

Preparation

1 To make the chicken forcemeat, cut the chilled chicken into pieces, and purée in a food processor. With the motor running, gradually add the chilled cream and the egg white. Season with salt and pepper.

2 Trim the ends off the morel stalks, and wash the mushrooms in several changes of water. Choose the 28 largest morels, remove the stalks, and wash the insides of the caps under cold running water. Drain on a cloth.

3 Fit a piping bag with a fine nozzle, fill it with the chicken forcemeat, and pipe the forcemeat into the morel caps. Place the filled morels on a plate, cover with plastic wrap, and refrigerate. Refrigerate the remaining forcemeat.

4 To make the filling for the timbales, halve the remaining morels. Heat 2 teaspoons butter in a small skillet, add the morels, and cook until soft. Deglaze with the Madeira, and reduce it completely away. Moisten with the whipping cream, bring up just to a simmer, remove from the heat, season, and set aside.

5 Using a small, pointed knife, bone out the frogs' legs by running the knife down both sides of the bones in the thighs and lower legs. Reserve the bones and trimmings. Melt a generous tablespoon of butter in a skillet, add the meat from the frogs' legs, and cook gently for 3 minutes. Season and set aside.

6 Mix together the frogs' legs and the morel cream and chop briefly to make them all the same size.

7 Chop the parsley sprigs and stir them in. Measure the volume of the mixture, and add an equal amount of the chicken forcemeat. Mix together and adjust the seasoning. Reserve the remaining chicken forcemeat.

8 Butter the molds, pack them with the mixture, and refrigerate.

9 Cook the perciatelli in abundant boiling salted water until al dente, taking care not to break the tubes. Drain.

10 Butter the bands of foil.

11 Cut the perciatelli into very even 1$^1/_2$-inch lengths, and arrange them in a 7-inch line on the foil bands. Spread a thin layer of plain chicken forcemeat over the perciatelli, and carefully place the foil bands in the refrigerator for at least 30 minutes.

12 Cut the asparagus tips to $^3/_4$ inch, cook for 2 to 3 minutes in boiling salted water, refresh in cold water, and drain.

13 Unmold the cylinders of forcemeat. Carefully wrap each one in a foil band, with the perciatelli on the inside, against the forcemeat. Press gently to help the perciatelli adhere, but take care not to break them. Replace in the refrigerator.

continued ▼

14 Pick off the chervil leaves, place in an airtight container, and keep cool.

15 To make the cream of frogs' leg, peel and finely chop the shallot, place in a skillet with the butter and the parsley stalks, and cook gently until translucent. Add the bones and trimmings from the frogs' legs, add the stock, and reduce over low heat by half. Add the whipping cream, and cook gently until it is thick enough to coat the back of a spoon. Season with cayenne, salt, and pepper, then strain through a colander lined with damp muslin or doubled cheesecloth. Keep cool.

Finishing Touches

1 Preheat the oven to 350°F.

2 Steam the asparagus tips to reheat them.

3 Arrange the timbales in an ovenproof dish, cover with a lid, and bake in the hot oven for 10 minutes.

4 Heat 2 teaspoons butter in a skillet until hot, add the filled morels, and sauté for 3 minutes.

5 Reheat the cream of frogs' legs, transfer to a blender (or use an immersion blender), and blend until foamy and thickened.

Presentation
Place a timbale in the center of each warmed plate. Remove the foil bands. Fan out 5 asparagus tips on each timbale. Pour a ribbon of cream of frogs' legs around each timbale, arrange 5 filled morels on the cream, and place an asparagus tip on top of each one. Place 2 filled morels on the timbales and garnish with chervil leaves.

Frogs' Legs en Papillote with Fresh Herb Risotto

Preparation

Serves 4 or 5

1 Using a small, pointed knife, bone out the frogs' legs by running the knife down both sides of the bones in the thighs and lower legs. You should have about 5 ounces of meat. Reserve the bones.

2 Slice the white and green parts of the green onions very finely.

3 Trim the small leek and slice the white and pale green parts very finely.

4 To make the stuffing, heat the butter in a nonstick skillet until very hot. Add the meat from the frogs' legs, season with salt and pepper, and stir for 30 seconds. Add the sliced green onions and leek, cook for another 20 seconds, then transfer the stuffing to a plate.

5 Put the skillet back on the heat, pour in half the cream, and reduce by half. Remove the skillet from the heat and vigorously stir in the egg yolk with a wooden spoon. Turn the heat down to very low, return the skillet to the heat, and let the sauce thicken, taking great care not to let it boil.

6 When the sauce is thick enough to coat the spoon, return the frogs' leg mixture to the skillet, stir for about 15 seconds, until it comes to a boil, then scoop the mixture into a bowl. Let cool to room temperature, then refrigerate.

7 Discard the outside leaves of the large leek, and cut off the dark and light green parts of the next four leaves. Cook these for 3 minutes in boiling salted water, refresh in cold water, and lay the leaves flat on a cloth. Tightly roll the leaves lengthwise like cigars, and cut them into strips about 1/6 inch wide. Unroll the strips, and shorten them to 6 inches. They will be used to tie up the papillotes.

8 Take the white part of the leek, halve it lengthwise, and cut into 2-inch lengths. Lay these out flat on the work surface, and cut into wafer-thin julienne; you will need 1/2 cup of julienne. Place in an airtight container, and keep cool.

9 To make the sauce, peel the shallot, chop it very finely, and place in a saucepan with 1 tablespoon of the clarified butter. Cook over medium heat until translucent, then add the reserved frogs' leg bones and cook gently for 2 minutes. Add the chicken stock, and simmer until reduced by half, keeping the heat low. Add the remaining cream and stir until slightly reduced and syrupy. Press the contents of the pan through a fine sieve into another saucepan, adjust the seasoning, and set aside.

10 Cut each sheet of phyllo into a 5 by 6-inch rectangle, and brush with a little clarified butter. Spoon a line of stuffing the size of your thumb along one of the longer sides, and roll up the phyllo like a cigarette. Tie the ends with the leek strips. Place the papillotes on a plate, cover with plastic wrap, and refrigerate.

11 Finely snip the chives and parsley, place in an airtight container, and keep cool.

48 frogs' legs
2 green onions
1 small leek
2 tablespoons unsalted butter
Salt and freshly ground pepper
1 1/4 cups whipping cream
1 egg yolk
1 large leek
1 large shallot
Scant 1/2 cup clarified butter
Scant 1/2 cup chicken stock
  (page 194)
8 to 10 sheets of phyllo
1/4 bunch chives
3 sprigs Italian parsley, finely chopped

Risotto
2 tablespoons unsalted butter
1/2 onion, chopped
Scant 3/4 cup arborio rice
About 2 cups hot chicken stock
  (page 194)
About 2 tablespoons whipping cream
1 1/2 tablespoons freshly grated
  Parmigiano-Reggiano

Oil, for deep-frying
All-purpose flour, for coating
2 tablespoons freshly shaved
  Parmigiano-Reggiano curls,
  for garnish

continued

Finishing Touches

1 Make the risotto, following the method in Rabbit Béatilles with Asparagus Risotto (page 34).

2 Preheat the oven to its highest temperature.

3 Heat the remaining clarified butter in a large nonstick skillet, add the papillotes, and fry them, turning them over until they are golden and crisp all over. Drain on paper towels.

4 At the same time, heat the oil in a deep-fat fryer or saucepan to about 340°F. Toss the leek julienne in flour, and deep-fry in the hot oil until nicely golden. Drain on paper towels, and place on the open oven door to keep warm.

5 Reheat the sauce, and stir in the chives and parsley.

Presentation
Divide the risotto between 4 large, warmed bowls, and place 2 papillotes on top, one resting on the other. Pour the sauce around, and garnish with the Parmigiano-Reggiano curls, and a sprig of parsley, if you have any left.

Sauté of Duck Foie Gras with Lentils

Preparation

1 Cut the foie gras into 1¼-inch cubes, place on a plate, cover with plastic wrap, and refrigerate.

2 Peel the cooked beet and cut it into ⅛-inch dice. Make a dressing with the white wine vinegar, peanut oil, salt, and pepper. Toss the beet in the dressing, and set aside.

3 To prepare the lentils, wash and drain them. Boil a saucepan of unsalted water, add in the lentils, blanch for 2 minutes, and drain. Peel the carrot and onion, and insert the clove into the onion. Discard the outer leaf of the leek. Return the lentils to the saucepan, add the vegetables and bouquet garni, and the bacon, if you like. Add 4½ cups cold water, quickly bring to a boil, then lower the heat, and gently cook the lentils for 25 to 30 minutes, until tender, but not bursting. Add salt 5 minutes before the end of the cooking time. When the lentils are cooked, remove the bacon, vegetables, and bouquet garni, and reserve the lentils, in their cooking liquid.

4 Cut off and reserve the tips of the chives. Chop the parsley leaves, and pick off the chervil leaves. Put all the herbs in separate airtight containers, and keep cool.

5 Wash the spinach leaves and spin them dry.

6 To make the sauce, peel and finely chop the shallot, and place in a small saucepan with the red wine vinegar and port. Reduce by three-quarters, add the brown veal stock, and reduce again by half. Add the hazelnut oil and balsamic vinegar, season with salt and pepper, and leave the sauce in the pan.

Finishing Touches

1 Season the cubes of foie gras, and toss lightly in flour.

2 Heat the olive oil in a nonstick skillet until very hot. Add the foie gras and sauté quickly for just long enough to color them attractively. Drain on paper towels.

3 Reheat the lentils.

4 Reheat the sauce, and blend briefly with a hand blender until smooth.

Serves 4

14 ounces raw duck foie gras
1 cooked beet
1 tablespoon white wine vinegar
2 tablespoons peanut oil
Salt and freshly ground pepper

Lentils

1⅛ cup Puy lentils
½ carrot
½ onion
1 clove
White part of ½ leek
1 bouquet garni (fresh thyme, parsley, and bay leaf)
2 ounces smoked bacon in large pieces (optional)
Salt

1½ tablespoons fresh chives
1½ tablespoons fresh Italian parsley,
1½ tablespoons fresh chervil
2 cups baby spinach leaves
1 shallot
3 tablespoons red wine vinegar
3 tablespoons port
3 tablespoons brown veal stock (page 197)
4 tablespoons hazelnut oil
3 tablespoons balsamic vinegar
All-purpose flour, for coating
1 tablespoon olive oil

Presentation
Place 2 large spoonfuls of lentils in the center of 4 warmed plates, and pile the cubes of foie gras in a mound on top. Arrange a ring of spinach leaves around, and scatter with diced beet. Pour the hot sauce over the foie gras, and garnish with chervil leaves, parsley, and chive tips.

Fish

Skate Wings with Mustard Butter, Cucumber, and Dill

Serves 4

Mustard Butter
$^1/_3$ cup unsalted butter, softened
2 tablespoons strong Dijon mustard
Juice of $^1/_2$ lemon
Ground cayenne pepper
Salt and freshly ground pepper

4 thick skate wings, 7 ounces each,
  skinned and boned
Salt and freshly ground pepper
$^1/_2$ to 1 European cucumber
2 tomatoes
1 shallot
$^1/_4$ cup unsalted butter
$^1/_4$ cup fish stock (page 198)
$^1/_4$ cup white wine
$^1/_4$ cup whipping cream
White wine vinegar
Dill sprigs, for garnish

Preparation

1 To make the mustard butter, combine the butter, mustard, lemon juice, cayenne, salt, and pepper, in a food processor, and pulse until well mixed.

2 Season the skate wings with salt and pepper, brush them with 3 tablespoons of the mustard butter, place on a plate, cover with plastic wrap, and refrigerate.

3 Peel the cucumber and, using a melon baller, scoop out mini-balls of flesh. Or, simply cut the cucumber into $^1/_6$-inch dice; in this case, you will only need $^1/_2$ of a cucumber.

4 Cut a shallow cross in the bases of the tomatoes. Boil a saucepan of water, plunge in the tomatoes for 15 seconds, and immediately transfer them into cold water. Peel and seed the tomatoes, and cut the flesh into tiny dice. Place in an airtight container, and keep cool.

5 To make the sauce, peel and finely chop the shallot, put it in a small saucepan with 2 teaspoons of the butter, and cook over medium heat until translucent. Add the fish stock and wine, and reduce by half. Strain into another saucepan to eliminate the shallot, add the cream, bring up to a simmer and cook for 30 seconds, then remove from the heat and set aside.

Finishing Touches

1 Reheat the cucumber balls or diced cucumber in $1^1/_2$ tablespoons of the butter. Add the diced tomatoes, and season. Remove from the heat.

2 Reheat the sauce over very low heat, and whisk in some mustard butter to thicken it. Do not boil. Adjust the seasoning with salt and pepper, and "lift" with a dash of vinegar. Remove from the heat.

3 Season the skate wings, and brush with remaining mustard butter.

4 Heat the remaining butter in a large nonstick skillet, and pan-fry the skate wings for 30 seconds on each side.

Presentation
Place a skate wing in the center of each plate, pour a ribbon of sauce around, and scatter the tomato and cucumber over the top. Garnish with sprigs of dill.

Golden Monkfish Tails with Sesame Seeds and Curried Winter Vegetables

Serves 4

2 carrots
2 turnips
$^{1}/_{2}$ celeriac (celery root)
12 cauliflower florets
White part of 1 leek
1 red bell pepper

Curry Sauce
1 tablespoon clarified butter
$^{1}/_{4}$ cup apple, cut into $^{1}/_{4}$-inch dice
$^{3}/_{4}$ cup mirepoix (mixed carrot, celery,
   and onion, cut into $^{1}/_{4}$-inch dice)
$^{1}/_{2}$ bay leaf
1 level tablespoon strong Madras
   curry powder
$^{3}/_{4}$ cup chicken stock (page 194)
Scant 1 cup milk
Scant $^{1}/_{2}$ cup whipping cream
Juice of $^{1}/_{2}$ lemon

1 unblemished savoy cabbage leaf,
   for the garnish
1 tablespoon clarified butter
4 pieces of monkfish tail on the bone,
   $1^{1}/_{4}$ inches thick, 5 ounces each
Salt and freshly ground pepper
$^{1}/_{4}$ cup flour
1 egg yolk
1 tablespoon whipping cream
$1^{1}/_{2}$ tablespoons sesame seeds
$^{1}/_{2}$ cup unsalted butter
1 level tablespoon strong Madras
   curry powder
Oil, for deep-frying
Juice of $^{1}/_{2}$ lemon

Presentation
Decorate the bottom of 4 warmed plates with zigzags
of the 2 different sauces. Put the vegetables to one
side, and place the monkfish in the center. Scatter the
deep-fried leek over the fish, and garnish with a piece
of the dried cabbage leaf.

Preparation

1 Peel the carrots, turnips, and celeriac, and pare them into narrow olive shapes, $1^{1}/_{2}$ inches long, or cut into $^{1}/_{2}$-inch cubes. Put them and the cauliflower in a cool place.

2 Halve the leek lengthwise, wash, and drain. Cut each half into $2^{1}/_{2}$-inch chunks, pile up the leaves from each chunk, and shred into very fine julienne. Keep in a cool place.

3 Preheat the oven to 175°F.

4 To make the red bell pepper jus, halve, seed, and remove the white ribs from the pepper. Slice the pepper finely and cook for 5 minutes in $^{1}/_{4}$ cup boiling salted water. Purée in a blender, and press through a fine sieve. Return the purée to the saucepan, and reduce to 2 tablespoons. Set aside.

5 To make the curry sauce, heat the clarified butter in a saucepan, add the apple, mirepoix, and bay leaf, season with salt and pepper, and sauté until lightly colored. Sprinkle with the curry powder, mix, and let it scorch just slightly on the bottom of the pan, then moisten with the chicken stock and milk. Simmer until the vegetables are tender. Purée the mixture in a blender, then press it through a fine sieve back into the saucepan, and reduce by half. Stir in the cream, adjust the seasoning, add a few drops of lemon juice, and set aside.

6 Brush the cabbage leaf with a little of the clarified butter, place on a baking sheet, and place in the preheated oven until just golden. Watch carefully, because it will quickly dry out, and you must remove it before it turns brown. Set aside.

7 Season the pieces of monkfish, and coat lightly with flour.

8 Mix the egg yolk and cream in a cup to make an eggwash, brush it over the fish, then lightly sprinkle one side with the sesame seeds. Place on a plate, cover with plastic wrap, and refrigerate.

Finishing Touches

1 Heat 2 tablespoons butter in a skillet, and add the vegetables and cauliflower. Cook gently over medium heat for a few minutes, stirring continuously, then sprinkle with the curry powder, and mix well to coat all the vegetables. Add a scant $^{1}/_{2}$ cup water, stir, and simmer the vegetables quickly until still just slightly firm.

2 Heat the frying oil to 350°F, and deep-fry the leek julienne until crisp. Drain on paper towels.

3 Reheat the red bell pepper jus over low heat, and whisk in $^{1}/_{4}$ cup butter to thicken. Season with salt, pepper, and a few drops of lemon juice.

4 Reheat the curry sauce.

5 Heat the remaining clarified butter in a nonstick skillet, add the monkfish, sesame-side down, and fry gently until golden. Turn the fish over and fry for 4 to 5 minutes total, until the fish is golden brown all over. Add the remaining butter to the skillet, heat, and keep basting the fish with the foaming butter for 1 minute.

Aiguillettes of John Dory with Ginger
and Tarragon Butter Sauce

Serves 4

5 ounces fresh ginger

4 John Dory fillets, 5 ounces each,
    halved lengthwise to make 8 strips
    (aiguillettes)

Ground cayenne pepper

Salt and freshly ground pepper

2 tablespoons whipping cream

1 tablespoon all-purpose flour

1 sprig tarragon

1 shallot

6 tablespoons unsalted butter, very
    cold and cubed

$^1/_4$ cup white wine

$^1/_4$ cup fish stock (page 198)

5 tablespoons clarified butter

Preparation

1 Peel the ginger, and reserve the peelings. Chop or grate $^1/_5$ of the ginger, and cut the rest into very fine julienne. Wrap the julienne in plastic wrap and refrigerate.

2 Season the fish strips with cayenne, salt, and pepper, brush them with 1 tablespoon of the cream, and coat with flour. Sprinkle the chopped or grated ginger over one side only, and press down to help it adhere to the fish. Place on a plate, cover with plastic wrap, and refrigerate.

3 Pull off the tarragon leaves, and chop them finely. Place in an airtight container, and keep cool.

4 To make the butter sauce, peel and finely chop the shallot, and place in a small saucepan with 2 teaspoons of the cold butter. Cook over medium heat until translucent. Add a few ginger peelings, the remaining 1 tablespoon of cream, the wine, and fish stock, and reduce to 2 tablespoons. Pass through a fine sieve into a clean saucepan, and set aside.

Finishing Touches

1 Heat 3 tablespoons of the clarified butter in a small skillet until very hot, add the ginger julienne, and sauté until pale golden and crisp. Drain on paper towels.

2 Reheat the butter sauce, increase the heat to high, and whisk in the cubes of cold butter, one at a time stirring. Season with cayenne, salt, pepper, and a few drops of lemon juice. Stir in the chopped tarragon and remove from the heat.

3 Heat the remaining 2 tablespoons of clarified butter in a nonstick skillet until very hot. Add the John Dory strips, ginger-side down, and cook for 50 seconds. Turn the fish over, and cook on the other side for 20 seconds. Drain on paper towels.

Presentation
Arrange 2 strips on each warmed plate. Pile a small
dome of fried ginger julienne on top, and pour a ribbon
of sauce all around.

Roast Turbot à la Boulangère
with Caper Butter

Preparation

Serves 4

1 Peel the potatoes, and trim them into even-shaped cylinders, then slice very thinly on a mandoline or in a food processor. Pat dry with a cloth, then lay them in overlapping circles to form four 3-inch rounds (galettes).

2 Heat 2 tablespoons of the clarified butter in each of 2 nonstick skillets. Using a spatula, carefully place 2 potato galettes in each skillet, season with salt, and brown on both sides. Remove the galettes with the spatula, and place on a buttered baking sheet.

3 Cut a cross in the base of the tomato, drop it into a saucepan of boiling water for 15 seconds, then immediately plunge it into cold water. Skin the tomato, halve, seed, and cut the flesh into tiny dice. Cover with plastic wrap, and keep cool.

4 Peel the green onion and slice the white part very finely. Cover with plastic wrap, and keep cool.

5 Pull off the Italian parsley leaves. Divide the curly parsley into small sprigs. Remove the stalks from the basil leaves, put all of these herbs in an airtight container, and keep cool.

6 Finely snip the chives, put them in a separate airtight container, and keep cool.

7 Season the turbot fillets with cayenne, salt, and pepper, brush them with the cream, then coat lightly with flour. Place on a plate, cover with plastic wrap, and refrigerate.

Finishing Touches

1 Preheat the oven to 475°F.

2 Heat the remaining 2 tablespoons of the clarified butter in a nonstick skillet. Put in the turbot fillets and cook for 2 minutes on each side, basting them with the butter. Add 2 tablespoons of the whole butter, and cook for another minute on each side, basting with the butter constantly. Lift out the fillets and drain on paper towels.

3 Discard the butter from the skillet, and replace it with the remaining 2 tablespoons fresh, whole butter. When the butter is hot, add the sliced green onion, stir until the butter is foaming, then add the capers and diced tomato. Pour in the vinegar to stop the cooking, remove the skillet from the heat, and season with salt and pepper.

4 When the oven is hot, put in the baking sheet with the potato galettes and leave them just until warm and crisp.

5 Heat the frying oil to 300°F in a deep-fat fryer, add all the herbs except the chives, and fry until crisp. Drain on paper towels.

4 even-sized small new potatoes
6 tablespoons clarified butter
Salt
1 tomato
1 small green onion
2 sprigs Italian parsley
2 sprigs curly parsley
12 fresh basil leaves
1/2 small bunch chives
4 middle-cut turbot fillets,
    5 ounces each
Ground cayenne pepper
Freshly ground pepper
1 tablespoon whipping cream
1 tablespoon all-purpose flour
4 tablespoons unsalted butter
1/2 cup capers, drained
2 tablespoons white wine vinegar
Oil, for deep-frying
2 pinches of pink peppercorns

Presentation
Put a potato galette in the center of each warmed plate. Place the fish on top, and coat with the caper butter. Garnish with fried herbs, and scatter the chives and pink peppercorns over the plates.

Grilled Turbot Steaks with Red Onion Compote and Pistachio Emulsion

4 thick turbot steaks, cut from the top
    fillets and skinned, 5 ounces each
Ground cayenne pepper
1 tablespoon grapeseed oil
Salt and freshly ground pepper

Red Onion Compote

3 red onions
1/4 cup red wine vinegar
About 1 1/2 cups full-bodied red wine
1 1/2 cups water
4 tablespoons honey
2 teaspoons unsalted butter

Pistachio Emulsion

4 tablespoons pistachio oil
2 tablespoons lemon juice

4 small leeks
1/8 cup shelled pistachio nuts, skinned
2 tablespoons unsalted butter
Red wine vinegar
3 tablespoons spiced jus (page 200)
1 tablespoon balsamic vinegar
2 pinches of coarsely ground pink
    peppercorns

Preparation

1   Season the turbot steaks with cayenne, salt, and pepper, and brush lightly with grapeseed oil. Place on a plate, cover with plastic wrap, and refrigerate.

2   To make the red onion compote, peel and slice the onions. Place in a saucepan with the vinegar and enough wine to barely cover. Cook gently for about 30 minutes, until all the liquid has evaporated. Add the water and honey, and continue to cook gently for another 10 minutes, making sure that the onions do not stick to the bottom of the pan. Add the butter, season with salt and pepper, mix well, and set aside.

3   To make the pistachio emulsion, combine the pistachio oil and lemon juice in a bowl, and mix with a hand blender until emulsified. Season with salt and pepper.

4   Discard the 2 outer leaves of the leek and all of the green part, which will not be used in this recipe. Wash the white part, blanch in boiling salted water for 3 minutes, refresh under cold running water, and drain. Cut on the diagonal into 3/4-inch lengths, and set aside.

5   Cut the pistachio nuts lengthwise into little batons, and set aside.

Finishing Touches

1   Heat a grill or a ridged griddle pan to medium-low.

2   Heat 1 tablespoon of the butter in a skillet, add the leeks, and roll them gently in the butter until heated through. Season with salt.

3   Reheat the red onion compote, and add a dash of red wine vinegar.

4   Pour the spiced jus into a small saucepan and bring to a boil. Add the balsamic vinegar, bring back to a boil, then turn off the heat, and whisk in the remaining 1 tablespoon of butter. Adjust the seasoning.

5   Place the turbot steaks on the not-too-hot grill or griddle pan, and cook for 2 1/2 minutes on each side, giving them a quarter-turn to make attractive crisscross markings.

Presentation
Spoon the red onion compote into the center of
4 warmed plates, and place the turbot on top. Scatter
on the pistachio batons and the leeks, pour a ribbon
of pistachio emulsion around, and dot with spiced jus.
Crumble some pink peppercorns over the plates.

Pan-Fried Royal Sea Bream with Artichokes, Fennel, and Saffron Onions

Serves 4

1 (3-pound) royal sea bream
  (daurade), scaled and cleaned

1 sprig thyme

2 sprigs dill

12 small violet artichokes

Juice of 1 lemon

1 large bulb fennel

1/2 onion

2/3 cup extra virgin olive oil

Pinch of ground saffron

Salt

1 large tomato

1/2 clove garlic

1 shallot

Freshly ground pepper

12 black olives

Chile Aïoli

1/2 red birdseye or serrano chile

1 clove garlic

1 egg yolk

Scant 1/2 cup extra virgin olive oil

Preparation

1 Cut off the fins from the sea bream, and put the thyme and 1 sprig of the dill inside the fish. Pick off the leaves from the rest of the dill and reserve them for the garnish. Delicately score the skin with crisscross incisions, place the fish on a plate, cover with plastic wrap, and refrigerate.

2 Cut the artichoke stalks to 1 1/2 inches, and cut off the top third of all the leaves. Peel the artichoke stems, turning them as you would an apple, and cut the stalks into a point. Cut each artichoke heart into 6 wedges, and drop them into a bowl of cold water acidulated with the lemon juice.

3 Remove and discard the large outer fennel leaves and the stalks. Cut the heart crosswise into very thin slices, place in an airtight container, and keep cool.

4 Peel the onion and cut crosswise into thin slices. Heat 2 tablespoons of the olive oil in a skillet, add the onion, and cook quickly until softened. Sprinkle with the saffron, season with salt, stir, then moisten with 3 tablespoons water, and cook gently until the water has evaporated. Remove from the heat, and set aside.

5 Cut a cross in the base of the tomato, plunge it into a saucepan of boiling water for 15 seconds, then immediately drop it into cold water. Skin, halve, seed, and cut the flesh into small dice.

6 To make the tomato concassé, chop the garlic and shallot very finely, put in a skillet with 1 tablespoon of the olive oil, and cook gently until the shallot is translucent. Add the diced tomato, season with salt and pepper, and continue to cook for 2 minutes, stirring continuously. Remove the skillet from the heat, and stir in 1 more tablespoon of the olive oil. Set aside.

7 Pit the olives and cut them lengthwise into thin batons. Set aside.

8 To make the chile aïoli, carefully remove the stem and seeds from the chile, and dice it very finely. Set aside. Halve the garlic and remove the green germ, put the garlic in a mortar, and crush it to a purée. Add the egg yolk, salt, and pepper, then make the aïoli like a mayonnaise, adding the olive oil in a steady stream, and pounding or whisking until smooth and thickened. If necessary, thin with a few drops of warm water, and stir in the chile, a little at a time, until the aïoli is spicy enough for your taste. Cover the mortar with plastic wrap, and set aside.

Finishing Touches

1 Preheat the oven to maximum heat.

2 Heat 3 tablespoons of the olive oil in a large, ovenproof skillet. Season the sea bream with salt and pepper, and place in the skillet. Set over high heat, and color on both sides.

3 When the fish is nicely browned, place the skillet in the hot oven for 8 minutes, turning the fish over after 4 minutes, and basting with the cooking oil often. To test whether the fish is ready, pull on the bone under one of the large fins near the head; you should be able to pull it out, but with some difficulty. Transfer the sea bream to a warmed serving platter, and place it on the open door of the oven.

4 Drain the artichoke wedges.

5 Sauté the fennel slices in 1 tablespoon olive oil, and season.

6 Add the remaining 2 tablespoons olive oil to the skillet in which you cooked the fish, heat, and add the artichokes. Cook quickly until lightly browned, and stir in the saffron onions at the last minute, just long enough to reheat them.

Presentation
On a platter, arrange the artichokes and fennel around the fish, scatter on the olive batons, and garnish with the reserved dill sprigs. Serve the tomato concassé and chile aïoli on the side.

Baked Fillets of Sea Bass with Zucchini and Caviar Sauce

Preparation

1 Spread 4 teaspoons of the butter over the fish fillets, and butter a plate. Put the fillets on the plate, cover with plastic wrap, and refrigerate.

2 Wash and dry the zucchini, but do not peel them. Pare off ⅛-inch strips of skin lengthwise all around, and cut these into ⅛-inch dice. Blanch in boiling salted water for 1 minute, refresh in cold water, drain, and set aside.

3 To make the sauce, peel the shallot and chop it very finely. Place in a small saucepan with 2 teaspoons of the butter, and cook over medium heat until translucent. Add the fish stock and lemon juice, and reduce by half. Add the cream, bring to a boil, then remove the pan from the heat, and season with cayenne, salt, and pepper. Press the sauce through a fine sieve into a clean saucepan, and set aside.

Finishing Touches

1 Preheat the oven to 350°F.

2 Gently mix 1 level tablespoon of the caviar with 1 teaspoon water to dilute it.

3 Season the sea bass fillets with salt, and cook in the preheated oven for 8 minutes.

4 Heat 4 teaspoons of the butter in a skillet, add the diced zucchini, and sauté quickly until hot. Season with salt.

5 Reheat the sauce. Over low heat, whisk in the remaining butter. Adjust the seasoning, and stir in the diluted caviar.

6 Remove the sea bass fillets from the oven and dab them with a buttered pastry brush to remove the albumen that has been released during cooking.

Serves 4

½ cup unsalted butter, softened
4 thick scallops of sea bass,
 about 5 ounces each
2 small zucchini
1 shallot
¼ cup fish stock (page 198)
¼ cup fresh lemon juice
2 tablespoons whipping cream
Ground cayenne pepper
Salt and freshly ground pepper
1¼ ounces caviar
Leaves from 1 stalk of lovage,
 for garnish

Presentation
Place the fillets on warmed plates (not too hot, or the fish will continue to cook). Coat with the sauce, and arrange the diced zucchini around. Top each fillet with a small quenelle of caviar, and garnish the plates with lovage leaves.

Wild Salmon with Sesame Seeds, Cabbage Fondue, and Spiced Jus

4 wild salmon fillets, 5 ounces each
2 egg yolks
Ground cayenne pepper
Salt and freshly ground pepper
$^1/_4$ cup sesame seeds

Cabbage Fondue
1 head savoy cabbage
1 green onion
1 tablespoon extra virgin olive oil
Scant $^3/_4$ cup vegetable bouillon
  (page 194)

Spiced Jus
1 shallot
1 tablespoon grapeseed oil
1 teaspoon *ras-el-hanout* (North
  African spice mix)
Scant $^1/_2$ cup red wine
1 tablespoon balsamic vinegar
2 tablespoons soy sauce
Scant $^1/_2$ cup fish stock (page 198)
1 tablespoon cornstarch (if necessary)

$1^1/_2$ tablespoons unsalted butter
2 tablespoons grapeseed oil
Sprigs of fresh herbs, such as
  rosemary and curly parsley, for
  garnish

Preparation

1 Cut the salmon fillets crosswise into $1^1/_4$-inch-wide strips.

2 Put the egg yolks in a cup, whisk lightly, and season with cayenne, salt, and pepper. Brush this mixture over the skin side of the salmon strips, sprinkle with sesame seeds, and press gently to help them adhere. Place on a plate, cover with plastic wrap, and refrigerate.

3 To make the cabbage fondue, discard the outer cabbage leaves, and separate the remaining leaves. Blanch the leaves for 2 minutes in boiling salted water, and refresh in cold water. Cut out the large central ribs, and drain the leaves, pressing them between your hands to eliminate all the water.

4 Peel and finely chop the white and green parts of the green onion, place in a sauté pan with the olive oil, and cook over medium heat until translucent. Add the cabbage leaves, season with salt and pepper, add the vegetable bouillon, and continue to cook until the cabbage is tender and melting. Remove the pan from the heat, and set aside.

5 To make the spiced jus, peel and finely chop the shallot, put it in a small saucepan with the grapeseed oil, and cook over medium heat until translucent. Add the *ras-el-hanout,* pour in the red wine, and stir to deglaze, then add the balsamic vinegar, soy sauce, and fish stock. Increase the heat, and reduce to a scant $^3/_4$ cup. If the jus seems too liquid, thicken it with the cornstarch mixed with 1 tablespoon cold water. Press the jus through a fine sieve into a clean saucepan, and set aside.

Finishing Touches

1 Reheat the cabbage fondue with a generous tablespoon of butter.

2 Reheat the spiced jus.

3 Heat 2 tablespoons grapeseed oil in a nonstick skillet until very hot. Add the salmon strips, skin-side-down, leave to color for 1 minute, then turn them over, and cook for 40 seconds on the other side. Remove from the skillet and drain on paper towels.

Presentation
Pile 2 spoonfuls of cabbage fondue in a dome in the center of warmed plates. Lean the salmon strips around and against the cabbage, and pour the spiced jus around. Garnish with a sprig or two of fresh herbs.

Spiced Fillet of Monkfish with Mustard Sauce

Serves 4

1 pound 2 ounces monkfish, cut
  from the center of the fillet

5 tablespoons whipping cream

Salt

2 tablespoons mixed spice (page 200)

1 tablespoon all-purpose flour

1 small carrot

1/4 celeriac (celery root)

1 shallot

1/2 cup unsalted butter, softened

1/4 cup white wine

1/4 cup fish stock (page 198)

2 tablespoons clarified butter

1 tablespoon Dijon mustard

Freshly ground pepper

2 teaspoons finely snipped fresh
  chives

Chervil leaves, for garnish

Preparation

1 Brush the monkfish with 2 tablespoons of the cream, season with salt and the mixed spice, and dust lightly with flour. Place on a plate, cover with plastic wrap, and refrigerate.

2 Peel the carrot and celeriac, and dice very finely. Set aside.

3 To make the mustard sauce base, peel and finely chop the shallot. Put it in a skillet with 2 teaspoons of the butter, and cook over medium heat until translucent. Add the diced carrot and celeriac, and cook for 1 minute, stirring. Add the wine and fish stock, and reduce by half. Add the remaining 3 tablespoons cream, bring to a boil, season, and remove from the heat.

Finishing Touches

1 In a skillet large enough to hold the monkfish, heat the clarified butter until very hot. Add the monkfish, and sear for 5 minutes, turning it over halfway through.

2 Pour off and discard the clarified butter from the skillet, replace it with 1/4 cup of the whole butter, and continue to cook for 7 to 8 minutes over very low heat, constantly basting the monkfish with the foaming butter. Do not let the fish brown.

3 Reheat the mustard sauce base. Over low heat, whisk in the remaining whole butter, then vigorously whisk in the mustard. Season with salt and pepper, and stir in the chives.

4 Transfer the monkfish to a carving board, and cut into 1/2-inch slices.

Presentation
Spread the hot mustard sauce over the bottom of
4 warmed plates, and arrange the slices of monkfish
on top. Garnish with chervil leaves.

72

Red Mullet Fillets with Orange Sauce

Preparation

1 Run your finger along the flesh side of the fish fillets, from tail to head, and remove all the small bones you can feel, using tweezers. Put the fillets on a plate, cover with plastic wrap, and refrigerate.

2 Rinse and drain the fish backbones and heads, and cut them into $^3/_4$-inch pieces.

3 Cut a cross in the base of one of the tomatoes, plunge into boiling water for 15 seconds, then immediately drop into cold water. Peel and seed the blanched tomato, and cut the flesh into tiny dice. Place in a skillet with $^1/_2$ tablespoon of the olive oil, cook gently until soft, season with salt and pepper, and set aside. Cut the second tomato into large dice, without peeling it.

4 Scrub the orange under hot water, and sponge dry. Pare off two $1^1/_4$-inch-wide strips of zest, remove any white pith from the underside, and cut the strips lengthwise into the thinnest-possible julienne. Place in an airtight container, and keep cool. Squeeze the orange to make a scant $^1/_2$ cup juice.

5 Chop the anchovy fillet very finely, and set aside.

6 Peel and very finely chop the shallot.

7 To make the sauce, place the shallot and 1 tablespoon of the olive oil in a small saucepan, and cook until translucent. Add the fish backbones and heads, and sear for 2 to 3 minutes, stirring with a wooden spoon. Add the unpeeled diced tomato, the wine, and orange juice, and continue to cook gently for 5 minutes. Press the sauce through a fine sieve into a clean saucepan and continue to reduce until there is a scant $^1/_2$ cup liquid remaining. Add the vegetable bouillon, and reduce to only 4 tablespoons liquid. Finish by stirring in 3 tablespoons of the olive oil and a few drops of lemon juice, season, and set aside.

8 Chop the slice of pineapple and 2 of the basil leaves, place in an airtight container, and keep cool.

Finishing Touches

1 Season the red mullet fillets with cayenne, salt, and pepper, and dust lightly with flour.

2 Reheat the sauce, and stir in the chopped anchovy, pineapple, cooked diced tomato, and the orange zest julienne. Bring to a boil, adjust the seasoning, and finely snip the remaining 2 basil leaves over the top.

3 Heat the clarified butter in 1 or 2 skillets until very hot. Add the red mullet fillets, skin-side down, and cook for 40 seconds. Turn them over, and cook for 20 seconds on the other side. Immediately take them out of the skillet, or they will continue to cook, and drain on paper towels.

Serves 4

4 red mullets, 5 to 7 ounces each, scaled and filleted (reserve the heads and backbones)

2 small tomatoes

4$^1/_2$ tablespoons extra virgin olive oil

Salt and freshly ground pepper

1 orange

$^1/_2$ oil-packed anchovy fillet

1 shallot

Scant $^1/_2$ cup white wine

Scant $^1/_2$ cup vegetable bouillon (page 194)

Juice of $^1/_2$ lemon

$^1/_4$ of 1 slice of fresh pineapple

4 fresh basil leaves

Ground cayenne pepper

All-purpose flour, for coating

2 tablespoons clarified butter

Guérande *fleur de sel,* for garnish

Presentation
Coat the bottom of 4 warmed plates with sauce, arrange 2 red mullet fillets in a V on top, and sprinkle with a few flakes of *fleur de sel.*

Red Mullet Fillets with Black Olives, Potato Ravioli, and Herb Coulis

Serves 4

4 red mullets, 5 to 7 ounces each,
   scaled and filleted (reserve the
   heads and backbones)
1 small shallot
2 teaspoons olive oil
Scant ¹/₂ cup white wine
Scant ¹/₂ cup water

Potato Ravioli
1 very large bunch of fresh chervil
1 very large waxy potato (red or
   white rose)
1 egg yolk
3 tablespoons clarified butter

1 small eggplant
8 black olives
1 small tomato
¹/₂ red bell pepper
Tabasco sauce
Salt and freshly ground pepper
All-purpose flour, for dusting
1 tablespoon whipping cream
7 tablespoons clarified butter
Scant ¹/₂ cup herb butter (page 194),
   softened
Ground cayenne pepper
2 tablespoons snipped fresh chives

Preparation

1   Run your finger along the flesh side of the fish fillets, from tail to head, and remove all the small bones you can feel, using tweezers. Put the fillets on a plate, cover with plastic wrap, and refrigerate.

2   To make the fumet, wash the red mullet backbones and heads. Peel and finely chop the shallot, put it in a small saucepan with 1 teaspoon of the olive oil, and cook over medium heat until translucent. Add the fish backbones and heads, and cook, stirring, for 2 minutes. Add the wine and water, and continue to cook gently for 5 minutes. Press the fumet through a fine sieve into a clean saucepan, and reduce to 3 tablespoons. Set aside.

3   To make the potato ravioli, finely snip enough chervil leaves to obtain 20 teaspoons. Peel the potato, and using a mandoline or food processor, slice the widest part into 40 wafer-thin slices at least 1¹/₂ inches in diameter. Dry these in a cloth. Spread 20 slices on the work surface, and brush with egg yolk. Place 1 teaspoon chervil in the center, and cover with another slice of potato. Press each ravioli with the palm of your hand to make the two halves stick together, then use a 1¹/₂-inch fluted pastry cutter to cut them into perfect circles. Brush both sides of the ravioli with clarified butter, place on a plate, cover with plastic wrap, and set aside.

4   Cut the eggplant into ¹/₂-inch dice. Place in an airtight container, and keep cool.

5   Pit the olives, and cut the flesh into tiny dice.

6   Cut a cross in the base of the tomato, plunge into boiling water for 15 seconds, then immediately drop into cold water. Peel, seed, and cut the flesh into tiny dice. Pat dry with paper towels.

7   Peel the bell pepper with a swivel peeler, seed, and remove the white ribs, and cut the flesh into tiny dice.

8   Heat the remaining 1 teaspoon olive oil in a small nonstick skillet, add the diced bell pepper, and cook gently for 2 minutes, without coloring. Add the olives, a dash of Tabasco sauce, and the diced tomato, season with salt and pepper, remove from the heat, and set aside.

Finishing Touches

1   Season the diced eggplant with salt and pepper, dust very lightly with flour, then mix with just a little cream; they will look gluey.

2   Heat 3 tablespoons of the clarified butter in a skillet until very hot, add the eggplant, and sauté quickly until golden and crusted, then drain on paper towels.

3   To make the herb coulis, reheat the reduced fumet. Over low heat, whisk in the herb butter. Season with cayenne, salt, and pepper, then stir in the chives and remove from the heat.

4   Heat 2 tablespoons of the clarified butter in the skillet until very hot, add the potato ravioli, and sauté until golden and crisp. Drain on paper towels.

5   Season the red mullet fillets with cayenne, salt, and pepper, and dust the skin side very lightly with flour. Heat the remaining 2 tablespoons of clarified butter in the skillet, add the fillets skin-side down, and sear for 40 seconds. Turn them over, and sear for 20 seconds on the other side. Drain on paper towels.

Presentation
Spoon a circle of herb coulis into the center of 4 warmed plates, and arrange 2 red mullet fillets in a V on top. Spoon a little of the olive and tomato mixture alongside each fillet, and arrange the potato ravioli in a fan at the top of the plate. Scatter the diced eggplant over the plates.

Barely Cooked Trout with Spices and Deep-Fried Leeks

Preparation

1 Brush the trout with a little butter, place on a plate, cover with plastic wrap, and refrigerate.

2 Peel the bell peppers with a swivel peeler, seed and remove the white ribs, and cut the flesh into tiny dice. Heat 1 teaspoon of the butter in a skillet, add the diced peppers, and cook gently for 2 minutes. Set aside.

3 Discard the two outer leaves of the leek and all the green part. Halve the white part lengthwise, wash, and drain. Cut each half into 2½-inch pieces, lay them flat on the work surface, and cut into the finest possible julienne, lengthwise. Place in an airtight container, and keep cool.

Finishing Touches

1 Preheat the oven to 325°F.

2 Heat the oil to 158°F, and deep-fry the leek julienne until crisp. Drain on paper towels.

3 Bring the spiced jus to a boil, and whisk in the remaining butter. Add the diced bell peppers. Remove from the heat.

4 Put the trout fillets on a buttered baking sheet, and cook in the oven for 10 minutes. Remove them from the oven, and dab with a buttered pastry brush to remove the albumen that has risen to the surface.

Serves 4

4 middle-cut slices of fillet from a large trout, 5 ounces each, about 1¼ inches thick

¼ cup unsalted butter, softened

½ red bell pepper

½ green bell pepper

1 leek

Oil, for deep-frying

¾ cup spiced jus (page 200)

Crushed black peppercorns, for garnish

Pinch of pink peppercorns, for garnish

Presentation
Spoon the spiced jus over the base of 4 warmed plates, and arrange a trout fillet on top. Sprinkle crushed black peppercorns and crumbled pink peppercorns over the top, and garnish with the deep-fried leek julienne.

Grilled John Dory with Matelote Sauce, Shredded Cabbage, and Baby Cuttlefish

Serves 4

8 strips of John Dory, cut lengthwise
  from the fillets, 2$^{1}/_{2}$ ounces each
2 tablespoons grapeseed oil
Ground cayenne pepper
Salt and freshly ground pepper

Shredded Cabbage

1 pound savoy cabbage
2 ounces smoked bacon
1 green onion
2 tablespoons unsalted butter

Matelote Sauce

2 cloves garlic
2 shallots
4 tablespoons unsalted butter,
  softened
3 cups Pinot Noir
Scant $^{1}/_{2}$ cup fish stock (page 198)
Scant $^{1}/_{2}$ cup brown veal stock
  (page 197)

7 ounces very small baby cuttlefish
  or squid
4 Italian parsley sprigs, for garnish

Preparation

1   Rub the fish with a little grapeseed oil, and season with cayenne, salt, and pepper. Place on a plate, cover with plastic wrap, and refrigerate.

2   To make the shredded cabbage, separate the cabbage leaves, discard the outside leaves and large ribs, and blanch the inner leaves for 1 minute in boiling salted water. Refresh in cold water, and drain thoroughly.

3   Cut the bacon into very thin julienne (lardons).

4   Finely chop the white and green parts of the onion, place in a small airtight container, and keep cool.

5   Chop each drained cabbage leaf into 4 or 5 pieces, and place in a colander.

6   To make the matelote sauce, peel and finely chop the garlic and shallots, place in a saucepan with 1$^{1}/_{2}$ tablespoons of the butter, and cook over medium heat until the shallots are translucent. Pour in the wine, fish, and veal stocks, and reduce to a scant $^{1}/_{2}$ cup of liquid. Press the sauce through a fine sieve into a clean saucepan to eliminate the garlic and shallots, season with salt and pepper, and set aside.

7   Clean the cuttlefish or squid, and chop them very coarsely. Place in a bowl, cover with plastic wrap, and refrigerate.

Finishing Touches

1   To cook the shredded cabbage, put the bacon, onion, and butter in a nonstick skillet, and set over medium heat until the butter is foaming. Add the cabbage, season with salt and pepper, and mix well, then decrease the heat, and simmer for 8 to 10 minutes.

2   Heat a grill or griddle pan.

3   Reheat the matelote sauce. Over low heat, whisk in the remaining 2$^{1}/_{2}$ tablespoons of the butter to thicken the sauce. Adjust the seasoning and remove from the heat.

4   Dry the cuttlefish in a cloth, and season with cayenne, salt, and pepper.

5   In a small skillet, heat 1 tablespoon of the grapeseed oil until smoking, add the cuttlefish, and sauté for 20 seconds, then drain in a sieve.

6   Put the strips of John Dory skin-side down on the hot grill or griddle pan, and cook for 40 seconds, then turn over, and cook for 20 seconds on the other side. Transfer to a plate.

Presentation
Make a little dome of cabbage on one side of
4 warmed plates, and top each with cuttlefish. Spread
a circle of matelote sauce on the other side, arrange
2 strips of John Dory on top, and garnish with a sprig
of parsley.

Poached Sea Bass with Cockles and Lovage

Preparation

1   Rinse the cavity of the sea bass, wrap it in plastic wrap, and refrigerate.

2   Wash the cockles in several changes of water, as they are always full of sand.

3   Peel and chop the shallot.

4   Put the cockles in a saucepan with the shallot, parsley, thyme, and ³/₄ cup of the vegetable bouillon. Cover and place over high heat. After it boils, cook for about 1 minute, until the cockles have opened. Immediately drain the ones that have opened, and strain and reserve the cooking juice.

5   Reserve 20 cockles in their shells for the garnish. Shell the rest, debeard them, rinse in the cooking juice, and drain, reserving the juice.

6   Strain the juice again through a fine sieve lined with damp muslin or doubled cheesecloth to eliminate all the sand. Set aside.

7   Set aside all the cockles in ³/₄ cup of the vegetable bouillon.

8   Finely snip enough of the lovage leaves to make 2 teaspoons and reserve a small bunch of leaves for the garnish. Place in an airtight container, and keep cool.

Finishing Touches

1   Pour the remaining bouillon and the wine into a fish poacher, add the remaining lovage, and heat until just simmering. Add the sea bass, and cook for 10 to 12 minutes, keeping the liquid simmering, but not boiling. To check if the fish is cooked, pull out one of the bones from the large dorsal fin; it should just come away but not too easily.

2   Drain the fish, and remove the skin.

3   Pour a scant ¹/₂ cup of the cooking juice from the cockles and a scant ¹/₂ cup of the stock from cooking the sea bass into a small saucepan. Reduce by half, decrease the heat, and thicken the reduction by whisking in the softened butter. Add the drained, shelled cockles and the snipped lovage leaves, and season with cayenne, salt, and pepper. Remove from the heat.

Serves 4

1 (3-pound) sea bass, scaled and
   cleaned
1 pound 2 ounces fresh cockles
   in the shell
1 shallot
5 sprigs parsley
1 sprig thyme
1 gallon (16 cups) vegetable bouillon
   (page 194)
3 large branches of lovage
1 cup white wine
Scant ¹/₂ cup unsalted butter, softened
Ground cayenne pepper
Salt and freshly ground pepper

Presentation
Place the sea bass on a serving platter, and coat with
the buttery cockle sauce. Garnish the platter with the
reserved cockles in their shells and lovage leaves.

Fillets of Wild Salmon with Fennel Purée and Olive Oil Emulsion

Serves 4

4 pieces of wild salmon fillet with the
    skin, 1¼-inch thick, and about
    1-inch wide
Salt and freshly ground pepper
1½ tablespoons unsalted butter,
    softened
2 bulbs fennel
Scant ¾ cup fish stock (page 198)
Pernod or other pastis (optional)
Half recipe of confit tomatoes
    (page 203)
1 tablespoon fresh lemon juice
Scant ½ cup extra virgin olive oil
    (Maussane, if possible)
1 tablespoon finely chopped fresh dill
Guérande *fleur de sel*, for garnish
Coarsely crushed black pepper,
    for garnish

Preparation

1 Season the pieces of salmon with salt and pepper and butter them generously on both sides. Place on a baking sheet, cover with plastic wrap, and refrigerate.

2 Trim the fennel, slice it thinly, and cook in boiling salted water until tender. Drain thoroughly, place in a blender or food processor with ¼ cup of the fish stock, and purée. Press through a sieve into a clean saucepan. The purée should have the consistency of a sauce; thin it with a few more drops of fish stock, if necessary. Season with salt and pepper, and a dash of Pernod. Set aside.

3 Finely chop the confit tomatoes.

4 To make the olive oil emulsion, pour a scant ½ cup of fish stock into a small saucepan, and reduce to 2 tablespoons. Pour into a bowl, add the lemon juice, and gradually whisk in the olive oil to emulsify the sauce. Set aside.

Finishing Touches

1 Preheat the oven to 325°F.

2 Reheat the fennel purée.

3 Stir the chopped confit tomatoes and the dill into the olive oil emulsion, and season with salt and pepper.

4 Place the salmon in the oven, and bake for 10 minutes.

5 Remove from the oven, remove the skin, and delicately dab with a buttered pastry brush to remove the albumen that has come to the surface during cooking.

Presentation
Spoon a circle of fennel purée into the center of 4 plates, and encircle it with a band of olive oil emulsion. Place a piece of salmon in the center of the fennel purée, and season with *fleur de sel* and crushed pepper.

Spiced Cod Fillets à la Boulangère

Serves 4

3 even-sized red or white rose
    potatoes
4 cod fillets, 1½ inches thick
6 fresh chives
1 green onion
All-purpose flour, for coating
Salt
1 tablespoon mixed spice (page 200)
2 tablespoons whipping cream
4 tablespoons clarified butter
Scant 1 cup unsalted butter, softened
Scant ½ cup spiced jus (page 200)
4 sprigs Italian parsley, for garnish

Preparation

1   Peel the potatoes and slice into wafer-thin slices on a mandoline or in a food processor. Rinse, lift out of the water with your hands, and transfer to a bowl of clean water.
2   Place the cod fillets on a plate, cover with plastic wrap, and refrigerate.
3   Finely snip the chives, place in an airtight container, and keep cool.
4   Peel and slice the white and green parts of the onion into thin rounds. Place in an airtight container, and keep cool.

Finishing Touches

1   Drain the potatoes and dry them thoroughly with a cloth.
2   Dust the cod fillets very lightly with flour, season with salt and the mixed spice, brush with the cream, and flour them again.
3   Heat the clarified butter in 2 large skillets, add half of the potatoes to each, and sauté, separating the slices. When they are golden, pour off the excess fat from the skillets, and add half the sliced onion and 2 tablespoons of the whole butter to each pan. Continue to cook for 2 minutes, stirring, and taking care not to burn the onion. Season with salt, and drain on paper towels.
4   Place the cod fillets into one of the same skillets, and cook over high heat for 1 minute on one side. Pour off the fat, replace it with 2 tablespoons of the whole butter, and continue to cook the cod for 1 minute longer, basting it with the foaming butter.
5   Reheat the spiced jus, and whisk in the remaining 4 tablespoons whole butter over low heat to thicken it. Remove from the heat.

Presentation
Arrange the potatoes in the center of 4 warmed
plates, and place the cod fillets on top. Pour the sauce
around the potatoes and very lightly over the fish.
Sprinkle with snipped chives, and garnish with a sprig
of parsley.

Red Mullet Fillets with Tomato Bourride and White Haricot Beans

Preparation

1 Soak the beans overnight in cold water. The next day, rinse in several changes of water. Peel the onion, and stick it with the clove. Put the beans in a saucepan, cover with 3 cups of water, and add the onion and bay leaf. Bring to a boil, and cook very gently for about 1½ hours, until the beans are tender. Add seasoning halfway through. Leave the beans in their cooking liquid.

2 Run your finger along the flesh side of the fish fillets, from tail to head, and remove all the small bones you can feel, using tweezers. Place the fillets on a plate, cover with plastic wrap, and refrigerate.

3 To make the bourride, dice the fish fillet, and thinly slice the potato. Peel and chop the garlic and shallot, put them in a small saucepan with ½ tablespoon of the olive oil, and cook over medium heat until the shallot is translucent. Add the diced fish and sliced potato, season with the saffron, salt, and pepper, add the fish stock and water, and cook until the potato disintegrates. Purée in a blender or food processor, then press through a fine sieve. Season with a pinch of cayenne and the lemon juice, then emulsify the bourride like a mayonnaise by drizzling in the ⅓ cup olive oil, whisking continuously. Measure out ½ cup of the bourride, and keep the rest for another use; it is impossible to make a smaller quantity!

4 Finely chop the confit tomatoes and stir into the ½ cup bourride. Cover and keep cool.

5 Wash the herbs and divide into small sprigs. Carefully pat dry, place in an airtight container, and keep cool.

Finishing Touches

1 Reheat the beans, and adjust the seasoning. Drain thoroughly.

2 Lightly flour the skin side of the red mullet fillets, and season.

3 Place the grapeseed oil in a large nonstick skillet, and heat until very hot. Add the red mullet, skin-side down, and cook for 40 seconds. Turn the fillets over and cook for 20 seconds on the other side. Immediately remove them from the skillet, and place on a plate.

4 Heat the deep-frying oil to 300°F, and fry the herbs until crisp. Drain on paper towels.

Serves 4

Beans

1½ cups dried white haricot beans

1 small onion

1 clove

½ bay leaf

Salt and freshly ground pepper

4 red mullets, 5 to 7 ounces each, scaled and filleted, skin left on

Bourride

2 ounces white-fish fillets

¼ raw potato, peeled

1 clove garlic

½ shallot

⅓ cup extra virgin olive oil, plus ½ tablespoon

Pinch of ground saffron

Scant ½ cup fish stock (page 198)

¼ cup water

Ground cayenne pepper

5 drops of lemon juice

1 ounce confit tomatoes (page 203)

1 cup fresh tarragon, loosely packed

1 cup fresh Italian parsley, loosely packed

1 cup fresh curly parsley, loosely packed

1 cup fresh lovage, loosely packed

All-purpose flour, for coating

1 tablespoon grapeseed oil

Oil, for deep-frying

1 tablespoon chile oil (page 200), for garnish

Presentation

Spread a circle of bourride over 4 warmed plates, and arrange 2 red mullet fillets in a V on top. Make a small dome of drained haricot beans at the point of the V, and garnish with deep-fried herbs. Drizzle a little chile oil along the top of the fillets.

Tuna Fish Tournedos with Ratatouille and Green Peppercorn Vinaigrette

4 slices of ahi tuna, cut from the
   middle of the fillet, about
   1¼ inches thick

2 small zucchini

¼ eggplant

½ onion

1 clove garlic

½ red bell pepper

½ yellow bell pepper

2 tomatoes

Scant ½ cup extra virgin olive oil

1 sprig thyme

1 shallot

¼ cup fish stock (page 198)

5 fresh basil leaves

Salt and freshly ground pepper

2 tablespoons red wine vinegar

1 tablespoon green peppercorns,
   drained

Ground cayenne pepper

1 tablespoon grapeseed oil

Fresh herbs, for garnish (optional)

4 branches of green peppercorns
   (optional)

Coarsely cracked black pepper, for
   garnish

Preparation

1   Trim the tuna slices to make a round shape, like a tournedo. (The trimmings are not needed in this recipe, so keep them to make a tartare.) Place the tournedos on a plate, cover with plastic wrap, and refrigerate.

2   Wash and trim, but do not peel, the zucchini and eggplant, and cut them into ½-inch dice.

3   Peel the onion, and cut it into ½-inch dice. Peel and finely chop the garlic.

4   Peel both bell peppers with a swivel peeler, quarter, and remove the seed, and white ribs. Reserve one-fourth of the red bell pepper for the sauce, and cut the rest into ½-inch squares for the ratatouille.

5   Cut a cross in the base of the tomatoes, plunge them into boiling water for 15 seconds, then immediately drop them into cold water. Peel and seed them, and reserve half of a tomato for the sauce. Cut the rest of the flesh into ½-inch squares for the ratatouille.

6   To make the ratatouille, heat 2 tablespoons of the olive oil in a shallow saucepan until very hot, add the eggplant, and cook for 4 minutes, stirring continuously. Remove with a slotted spoon, and drain on paper towels. If necessary, add a little more olive oil to the saucepan, add the zucchini, and sauté for 4 minutes. Remove with a slotted spoon, and drain on paper towels. Add a little more olive oil if necessary to the saucepan, add the onion and red and yellow peppers, and cook for 4 minutes. Add the garlic, and cook for 1 minute longer, stirring. Remove the pan from the heat, and return the drained eggplant and zucchini. Pull off the thyme leaves, and scatter them over the contents of the pan. Set aside.

7   Cut the reserved red bell pepper and tomato into ⅛-inch dice (brunoise). Place the brunoise in an airtight container, and keep cool.

8   To make the sauce, peel and chop the shallot very finely, place in a small saucepan with 1 tablespoon of the olive oil, and cook over medium heat until translucent. Add the brunoise, and cook for another 2 minutes, until tender. Add the fish stock and reduce by half. Remove from the heat, and set aside.

9   Snip the basil leaves, place in a small airtight container, and keep cool.

Finishing Touches

1   Heat a grill or griddle pan until very hot.

2   Return the pan of ratatouille to the heat, add the tomato squares, season with salt and pepper, heat through, then stir in the basil.

3   Reheat the sauce, add the vinegar, and whisk in 1 tablespoon of the olive oil. Season with salt and pepper, and stir in the brunoise and the drained green peppercorns.

4   Season the tuna tournedos with cayenne, salt, and pepper, brush them with grapeseed oil, and grill for 2 minutes on each side, giving them a quarter-turn halfway through to make an attractive crisscross marking.

Presentation
Spoon the ratatouille into the center of 4 plates, and prop the tournedos at an angle against it. Spoon the sauce to one side. Garnish with a small bouquet of herbs and a branch of green peppercorns, if desired. Scatter a little cracked black pepper on the side of each plate.

Turbans of Sole in Shellfish Jus

Serves 4

2 sole, 1½ pounds each, skinned and filleted, or 4 filets of sole

¼ cup unsalted butter, softened

Ground cayenne pepper

Salt and freshly ground pepper

20 fresh cockles in the shell

12 mussels

20 large scallops in their shells, or use dry-pack or diver scallops and bought scallop shells

¼ cup white wine

2 baby leeks

6 fresh chives, for garnish

Scant ½ cup plus 1 tablespoon vegetable bouillon (page 194)

¼ cup herb butter (page 194), softened

1 tablespoon pink peppercorns, for garnish

Preparation

1   Roll up the sole fillets, lengthwise, like turbans, and place on a rimmed, buttered baking sheet. Brush the turbans with a little butter, season with cayenne, salt, and pepper, cover with plastic wrap, and refrigerate.

2   Wash all the shellfish thoroughly, and scrub the shells, if necessary.

3   Place the cockles and mussels in a saucepan with the wine, cover, and set over high heat for about 1 minute, until the shellfish have opened. Drain, reserving all the juices, then strain the juices through a sieve lined with damp muslin or doubled cheesecloth. Remove the top shells from the cockles and mussels, and place them, on the half-shell, in their strained juices.

4   Open the scallops, and clean and debeard them under running water. Place on a plate, cover with plastic wrap, and refrigerate.

5   Wash and trim the leeks. Halve them lengthwise, and keep only the green leaves for this recipe. Lay the leek greens flat on the work surface, open out, and cut into about 40 diamond shapes, about ½ inch on each side. Blanch in boiling salted water for 3 minutes, refresh in cold water, drain, and set aside.

6   Snip the chives, place in a small airtight container, and keep cool.

Finishing Touches

1   Preheat the oven to 350°F.

2   Remove the cockles and mussels from their juices.

3   Pour the juices and a scant ½ cup of the vegetable bouillon onto the baking sheet with the sole turbans, cover with aluminum foil, and cook in the oven for 8 to 10 minutes.

4   When the turbans are cooked, transfer them to a platter, and place on the open oven door to keep warm.

5   Pour all the cooking juices into a small saucepan, place over low heat, and whisk in the herb butter to thicken the sauce. When all of the butter is incorporated, add the scallops, cook for 30 seconds, then stir in the leek diamonds, the cockles, and the mussels. Remove from the heat, and season.

Presentation
Place a sole turban on each warmed plate. Divide the buttery sauce and shellfish between the plates. Sprinkle the chives and pink peppercorns over the plates.

Pan-Fried Sea Bass Scallops with
Potato Scales and Tarragon Jus

Preparation

1 Cut off the thin edge of the sea bass fillets, then cut each fillet into two attractive scallops.

2 Reserve a tarragon and parsley leaves for the garnish. Finely chop all the remaining parsley leaves with half of the remaining tarragon leaves, and reserve. Finely chop the rest of the tarragon and reserve separately.

3 Peel the potatoes, trim off the ends, and cut them into regular cylinders. Cut these into wafer-thin slices using a mandoline or food processor.

4 Brush the sea bass scallops with a little butter on what *was* the skin side. Season the buttered side with cayenne, salt, and pepper, and dust generously with the chopped tarragon and parsley mixture. Cover the herb-covered side only with potato slices, overlapping them to resemble scales. Place carefully on a plate, cover with plastic wrap, and refrigerate.

5 To make the acidulated jus base, peel and finely chop the shallot. Place in a small saucepan with the wine, and reduce to 4 tablespoons. Add the balsamic and red wine vinegars, and set aside.

Finishing Touches

1 Heat the clarified butter in a large, nonstick skillet until very hot. Carefully place in the sea bass scallops, potato-side down, and pan-fry for 4 to 5 minutes, until the potatoes are nicely golden. Immediately turn the scallops over, cook for no more than 30 seconds, and remove from the pan so that they do not continue cooking.

2 At the same time, reheat the jus base, and stir in the hazelnut and grapeseed oils. Emulsify the jus with a hand blender or in a standing blender, season, and add the chopped tarragon.

Serves 4

1 (3-pound) sea bass, scaled, filleted and skinned

1 cup fresh tarragon leaves

$\frac{1}{2}$ cup fresh Italian parsley leaves

10 ounces even-sized *ratte* potatoes

$1\frac{1}{2}$ tablespoons unsalted butter, softened

Ground cayenne pepper

Salt and freshly ground pepper

1 shallot

Scant $\frac{1}{2}$ cup white wine

1 tablespoon balsamic vinegar

1 tablespoon red wine vinegar

$\frac{1}{4}$ cup clarified butter

$\frac{1}{4}$ cup hazelnut oil

$\frac{1}{4}$ cup grapeseed oil

Presentation
Place the sea bass scallops in the center of 4 warmed plates, and pour the jus around. Garnish with the reserved sprigs of tarragon and parsley.

Sole on the Bone with Leeks and Tomato Jus

Serves 4

2 whole sole on the bone, about
　2 pounds each

20 small scallops, preferably dry-pack
　or diver

8 baby leeks, the width of your pinkie
　finger, cleaned

2 violet artichokes

Juice of 1/2 lemon

1 small onion

Scant 1/2 cup white wine

Salt and freshly ground pepper

2 tablespoons extra virgin olive oil

6 black olives

4 cherry tomatoes

1/4 cup fish stock (page 198)

Ground cayenne pepper

2 tablespoons whipping cream

All-purpose flour, for coating

2 1/2 tablespoons unsalted butter

Scant 1/2 cup herb butter (page 194),
　softened

2 tablespoons clarified butter

Small sprigs dill, for garnish

Presentation

Place the pieces of sole on warmed plates. Delicately pull out the base of the backbone, so that it is visible, but still attached to the flesh. Arrange an artichoke fan at one end, 2 leeks on one side, some leek diamonds and 5 scallops on the other side, and a spoonful of tomato jus opposite the artichoke. Dab some herb butter artistically on the plate, and scatter with the olives. Garnish with sprigs of dill.

Preparation

1   To prepare the sole, remove the heads, skin the fish, and lift off the white fillets (they will not be used in this recipe). Cut through the bones that run the length of one side of the backbone, leaving the top fillets attached, and cut off the outside "skirts" and tails with scissors. Divide both long pieces of sole into two equal parts (see photo opposite). If possible, ask your fishmonger to do this for you.

2   Open the scallop shells, if necessary, remove the scallops, and wash in cold water. Place on a plate, cover with plastic wrap, and refrigerate.

3   Remove the outermost 2 layers of the leeks, trim and wash them, cut them to 4 inches long, blanch for 3 minutes in lightly salted boiling water, refresh in cold water, and drain. Cut off the green tops of the leek leaves on the diagonal to make diamond shapes, place in an airtight container, and keep cool. Reserve the leek bottoms.

4   Shorten the artichoke stalks to 1 1/2 inches, and cut off the top third of the leaves. Peel the artichokes, turning them as you would an apple, and cut the stalks into points. Rub the artichoke bases and stalks with lemon juice. Peel the onion, and cut it into rounds. Lay the onions rounds in the bottom of a small saucepan, arrange the artichoke hearts on top, and pour in the wine and enough water to come halfway up the artichokes. Season with salt and pepper, and simmer gently for 30 minutes.

5   Halve the artichokes lengthwise (including the stalks), remove the chokes, and fan out the half-hearts, keeping them attached to the stalks. Brush a small skillet with 1 tablespoon of the olive oil, add the artichokes, cut-side up, and set aside.

6   Pit the olives, and cut the flesh into tiny dice. Set aside.

7   To make the tomato jus, cut a cross in the base of the tomatoes, plunge them into boiling water for 15 seconds, then immediately drop them into cold water. Peel, seed, and dice the flesh, then purée in a blender or food processor, and pass through a fine sieve. Pour the tomato pulp into a small saucepan, and reduce by half. Remove from the heat, stir in the remaining 1 tablespoon olive oil, and season. Set aside.

8   Pour the fish stock into a saucepan, reduce to 1 tablespoon, and set aside.

Finishing Touches

1   Season the pieces of sole with cayenne, salt, and pepper, brush them very lightly with the cream, then coat with flour.

2   Place the leek bottoms in a pan with 1 tablespoon water and 1 teaspoon of the butter, and reheat.

3   Place the leek diamonds in a small pan with 1 tablespoon water and 2 teaspoons of the butter, and cook for 3 to 4 minutes. They should still be firm. Season with salt and pepper.

4   Set the skillet containing the artichokes over high heat, and lightly brown the artichokes on both sides.

5   Reheat the tomato jus. If necessary, use a hand blender to bring it back together.

6   Reheat the reduced fish stock, and whisk in the herb butter to thicken. Season, remove from the heat, and cover the pan.

7   Heat the clarified butter in a nonstick skillet until fairly hot. Add the pieces of sole, and cook for 3 minutes. Turn over, add 4 teaspoons whole butter, and cook for 4 minutes more, basting continuously with the foaming butter. Remove the skillet from the heat, transfer the sole to a plate, and keep warm.

8   Season the scallops with salt and pepper, add them to the skillet in which you cooked the sole, and sauté for 20 seconds.

Shellfish

Lobster with Crisp Saffron-Flavored Belgian Endive

Serves 4 (as a starter)

2 live lobsters, 1 pound 2 ounces each
$1/4$ cup unsalted butter, softened
$3/4$ cup mesclun leaves
4 small Belgian endives
1 tablespoon English mustard
1 tablespoon walnut oil
$1^{1}/2$ tablespoons sherry vinegar
Salt and freshly ground pepper
$1/4$ cup lobster stock (page 196)
1 tablespoon wine vinegar
2 tablespoons extra virgin olive oil
14 fresh chives
1 teaspoon ground saffron
2 tablespoons peanut oil
Ground cayenne pepper
$1/2$ teaspoon saffron threads, for
    garnish

Preparation

1 Bring a large saucepan of salted water to a boil, and drop in the lobsters. Bring back to a boil and cook for $1^{1}/2$ minutes, then drain. Detach the claws and legs, and remove the meat. Remove and discard the heads, halve the tails lengthwise, and remove the black intestinal thread. Brush all the meat with butter, leaving the tails in the shells, place on a plate, cover with plastic wrap, and refrigerate.

2 Wash the mesclun, and spin it dry.

3 Pick off 24 good Belgian endive leaves, place in an airtight container, and keep cool.

4 To make the lobster vinaigrette, in a bowl, mix the mustard, walnut oil, sherry vinegar, salt, and pepper, and stir in the lobster stock. Set aside.

5 To make the olive oil vinaigrette, in a bowl, whisk together the wine vinegar, olive oil, salt, and pepper.

6 Reserve 8 whole chives, and finely snip the remaining 6. Place in an airtight container, and keep cool.

Finishing Touches

1 Season the endive leaves with $1/2$ teaspoon ground saffron, salt, and pepper, and coat them with 1 tablespoon of the peanut oil.

2 Heat the remaining 1 tablespoon peanut oil in a skillet, add the endive leaves, and sauté briefly. Place on paper towels.

3 Season the lobster meat with cayenne, salt, and the remaining $1/2$ teaspoon ground saffron.

4 Heat 2 tablespoons of the butter in a skillet until foaming, put in the lobster tails, shell-side down, and heat for 2 minutes. Turn them over, and heat for 1 minute on the other side. Remove the tails from the skillet. Or you may reheat the tails in the oven at 450°F.

5 Using the same butter, sauté the claw and leg meat for 1 minute. Remove them from the skillet.

6 Toss the mesclun in the olive oil vinaigrette.

7 Cut each half lobster tail into 4 pieces, and toss them in the lobster vinaigrette.

Presentation
In the center of each plate, reconstitute a half lobster tail into its original shape, shellside upward. Add the meat from one claw and some of the leg meat. Arrange a fan of Belgian endive leaves at the top end, and strew with mesclun. Prop 2 whole chives above the lobster tails, and scatter the snipped chives and saffron threads over the Belgian endive leaves. Drizzle the lobster vinaigrette around the edge.

Whole Poached Lobsters with
Tarragon Bouillon and Saffron Rouille

Serves 4 (as a main course; for a starter, serve ½ lobster per person, but do not change any of the other quantities)

4 live lobsters, 14 ounces each

1 tablespoon extra virgin olive oil

1 cup mirepoix (equal parts carrot, green part of a leek, and celery, cut into ¼-inch dice)

3 cloves garlic, unpeeled

2¼ cups vegetable bouillon (page 194)

1 whole birdseye or serrano chile

1 piece of orange zest, 1¼ by 2½ inches

1 bouquet garni (fresh thyme, parsley, and bay leaf)

1 carrot

2 celery

1 green part of a leek, washed

½ cup fresh tarragon leaves

½ cup unsalted butter, softened

Ground cayenne pepper

Salt and freshly ground pepper

4 tablespoons saffron rouille (page 203), for garnish

Preparation

1   Bring a large saucepan of salted water to a boil, and drop in the lobsters. Bring back to a boil and cook for 1½ minutes, then drain the lobsters. Detach the claws tails, and legs, place on a plate, cover with plastic wrap, and refrigerate.

2   To make the bouillon, remove the gritty sacs from the heads, then finely chop the heads, bodies, and legs. Put them in a saucepan with the olive oil, and cook gently for 3 to 4 minutes. Add the mirepoix and garlic, cook for another 3 minutes, then add the vegetable bouillon, chile, orange zest, and bouquet garni, and cook gently for 20 minutes. Press through a fine sieve lined with damp muslin or doubled cheesecloth.

3   Peel the carrots and celery. Cut them into ⅛-inch-thick slices, then into ½-inch triangles, and blanch the two vegetables separately in the boiling bouillon for about 3 minutes. Lift them out with a slotted spoon, drain, and set aside.

4   Separate the green leek leaves, and cut them into ½-inch triangles. Blanch in the bouillon until tender, remove with a slotted spoon, refresh in cold water, drain, and set aside.

5   Snip the tarragon leaves, place in an airtight container, and keep cool.

Finishing Touches

1   Bring the bouillon to a boil, drop in the unshelled lobster tails and claws, decrease the heat, and cook at a bare simmer for 5 minutes. Remove the lobster pieces, shell them, and keep warm.

2   Strain the bouillon into a saucepan and bring to a boil. Turn the heat down to low, and whisk in the butter to thicken. Season with cayenne, salt, and pepper, and add the vegetable triangles and tarragon.

Presentation
Place a lobster tail and two claws in 4 large warmed bowls. Pour the very hot lobster bouillon over, and garnish each serving with a tablespoon of saffron rouille.

Lobster Meunière with Petits Pois and Lovage Sauce

Preparation

1 Bring a large saucepan of salted water to a boil, and drop in the lobsters. Bring back to a boil and cook for 1½ minutes, then drain. Take off the heads, halve the tails lengthwise, and remove the black intestinal thread. Remove the meat from the claws and tail pieces. Place all the lobster meat on a plate, brush with a little butter, cover with plastic wrap, and refrigerate.

2 To make the optional garnish, scrape out the heads, and cut them 1½ inches below the end, where they join the body. Blanch them in boiling water until they turn red. Drain and reserve.

3 Bring a saucepan of water to a boil, add the petits pois, return to a boil, and drain immediately. Refresh in cold water, and drain again.

4 Reserve ¼ cup of the petits pois for the garnish.

5 Carefully dry the remaining petits pois with a cloth, and press them through the finest disk of a food mill or pulse in a food processor, then press firmly through a fine sieve to make a smooth purée. Place in a bowl, cover, and set aside.

6 To make the sauce base, cut the lovage stalk into chunks (reserving the leaves), place in a saucepan with the lobster stock, bring to a boil, and reduce to a syrupy consistency. Season with salt and pepper, add the Cognac and cream, press through a fine sieve, and leave in the saucepan.

7 Peel and finely chop the shallot, place in an airtight container, and keep cool.

8 Chop the lovage leaves, place in an airtight container, and keep cool.

Finishing Touches

1 Preheat the oven to 350°F.

2 Season the lobster tails and claws with cayenne, salt, and pepper.

3 Heat 2 tablespoons of the butter in a large ovenproof skillet, and add the lobster claws and half-tails, shell-side up. Add the shallot, cook for 30 seconds, then turn the lobster over, and transfer to the oven for 5 minutes.

4 Meanwhile, reheat the petits pois purée with 1½ tablespoons butter, and season.

5 Bring a small pan of water to a boil, add the reserved petits pois, and reheat for 20 seconds, then drain.

6 Reheat the sauce base over low heat, and whisk in 2 tablespoons of the butter to thicken. Add the lovage leaves, and season.

7 When the lobster tails are cooked, lift out three-fourths of the meat from the shells, without detaching it completely. Using a piping bag with a plain nozzle, pipe the petits pois purée into the empty part of the shells.

Serves 4 (as a main course; for a starter, serve ½ lobster per person, and halve the quantity of petits pois purée)

4 live lobsters, 14 ounces each
Scant ½ cup unsalted butter, softened
1 pound 2 ounces extra-fine frozen
  petits pois, still frozen
1 stalk of lovage
1 cup lobster stock (page 196)
Salt and freshly ground pepper
2 teaspoons Cognac
2 tablespoons whipping cream
1 large shallot
Ground cayenne pepper

Presentation
Place 2 halved lobster tails on each warmed plate, and garnish with the claws and heads (optional). Pour the sauce around, and scatter with the reserved whole petits pois.

Matelote of Lobster and Langoustines with Merlot Sauce

2 live lobsters, 14 ounces each

2¹/₂ tablespoons unsalted butter, softened

Merlot Sauce

2 shallots

¹/₂ bay leaf

Pinch of sugar

1¹/₄ cups Merlot

8 langoustine tails

8 baby leeks, the size of your pinkie finger

Mousseline Sauce

2 shallots, finely chopped

Scant ¹/₂ cup white wine

2 egg yolks

1 sprig dill

3 tablespoons unsalted butter, softened

Salt and freshly ground pepper

1 tablespoon clarified butter

Crushed pink peppercorns, for serving (optional)

Dill sprig, for serving

Preparation

1 Bring a large saucepan of salted water to a boil, and drop in the lobsters. Bring back to a boil and cook for 1¹/₂ minutes, then drain. Remove the heads, claws, and legs. Shell the claws and tails completely, and brush with butter. Place on a plate, cover with plastic wrap, and refrigerate.

2 Carefully remove the gritty sac from one of the heads, and chop or crush the head completely.

3 To make the Merlot sauce, peel and finely chop the shallots. In a saucepan, combine the crushed lobster head, shallots, bay leaf, sugar, and Merlot. Place over medium heat, skimming the surface, and reduce to a scant ¹/₂ cup. Set aside.

4 Shell the langoustine tails, and remove the black intestinal thread. Place the tails on a plate, cover with plastic wrap, and set aside.

5 Wash the leeks thoroughly, halve horizontally where the white meets the green, and shorten the green part to 2 inches. Finely shred the green part, cook them in boiling salted water for 5 minutes, refresh in cold water, and drain. Shorten the white parts to 1¹/₄ inches, arrange the leeks in a small baking dish, cover with plastic wrap, and set aside.

6 To make the mousseline sauce base, put the chopped shallots in a small saucepan with the wine and bring to a lively boil for 3 minutes. Press through a sieve to eliminate the shallot, return to the pan, and set aside.

7 Finely snip the dill leaves, place in an airtight container, and keep cool.

Finishing Touches

1 Preheat the oven to 400°F.

2 Put a small piece of butter on each half lobster tail and claw, season with salt and pepper, and place in a baking dish.

3 Dot a few flakes of butter over the leeks.

4 Place the lobster and leeks in the oven for 3 minutes.

5 Heat the mousseline sauce base over very low heat, or in a bain-marie, add the egg yolks, and whisk until the sauce begins to thicken. Still whisking, add the softened butter, then the dill, and season. Remove the pan from the heat.

6 Season the langoustines. Heat the clarified butter in a skillet, add the langoustines, cook for 30 to 40 seconds on each side, and immediately drain on paper towels.

7 Briefly reheat the shredded leek greens.

Presentation

Pour a spoonful of Merlot sauce into the center of 4 warmed plates, and spread it into a small circle, without covering the entire surface. Arrange 2 langoustines in a V on the sauce, at the bottom right of the plates. Place 2 leeks at the head of the langoustines. Cut the halved lobster tails into 6 slices, and re-form them, arranging them at an angle opposite the langoustines. Put a spoonful of mousseline sauce between the lobster and the langoustine. Sprinkle the leek greens and crushed pink peppercorns over the plates. Garnish with a sprig of dill.

Langoustines with Chile Aïoli and
Sesame-Coated Mussels

Serves 4

2 very large langoustines

40 mussels

1 onion, peeled and chopped

Scant ¹/₂ cup white wine

2 to 3 tablespoons all-purpose flour

1 egg, lightly beaten

¹/₄ cup sesame seeds

Chile Aïoli

2 cloves garlic, peeled, halved, and
    green germ removed

2 egg yolks

Salt and freshly ground pepper

²/₃ cup extra virgin olive oil

Lemon juice

1 whole birdseye or serrano chile

4 tablespoons grapeseed oil

Ground cayenne pepper

4 sprigs cilantro, for garnish

Preparation

1   Shell the langoustines, leaving on the last ring of shell at the tail. Use the tip of a small knife to remove the black intestinal thread. Place the langoustines on a plate, cover with plastic wrap, and refrigerate.

2   Scrub the mussels under running water. Put them in a saucepan with the onion and wine, cover, and set over high heat for about 1 minute, shaking the pan several times, until the mussels have opened. Drain, let cool, then carefully take them out of their shells. Place on a cloth to dry.

3   Put the flour, egg, and sesame seeds into separate bowls. Coat the mussels first in the flour, then in the egg, and finally in the sesame seeds. Place on a plate, cover with plastic wrap, and refrigerate.

4   To make the chile aïoli, crush the garlic to a paste in a mortar, add the egg yolks, and season with salt and pepper. Whisk in the olive oil in a very thin stream, to make a thick, mayonnaise-like sauce. If the consistency is too thick, dilute the aïoli with a tablespoon of lukewarm water. Stir in a few drops of lemon juice. Stem and open up the chile, scrape out all the seeds, and mince and crush the chile into a purée. Add as little or as much as you wish to the aïoli, cover, and keep cool.

Finishing Touches

1   Heat 3 tablespoons of the grapeseed oil in a skillet until very hot. Add the mussels, and fry until crisp all over. Drain on paper towels.

2   Season the langoustines with cayenne, salt, and pepper. Heat the remaining grapeseed oil in the skillet until very hot, add the langoustines, and cook for 50 seconds on each side. Immediately remove them from the skillet, and drain on paper towels.

Presentation

Arrange 3 langoustines in a fan at the top of each warmed plate, with the tails toward the center. Spoon a semicircle of aïoli below, and scatter the mussels on top. Garnish with a sprig of cilantro.

Sautéed Langoustines with Rosemary Cream and Lentils

Preparation

1 Cook the lentils, following the recipe in Sauté of Duck Foie Gras with Lentils (page 57), and leave them in their cooking liquid.

2 Remove the langoustine heads, if necessary. Shell the tails, leaving the last two rings of shell attached at the tail. Use the tip of a small knife to remove the black intestinal thread. Place the langoustines on a plate, cover with plastic wrap, and refrigerate.

3 Put the langoustine stock in a saucepan with 1 sprig of the rosemary, and reduce by half. Add the cream, and cook gently until the sauce is very creamy, and thick enough to coat the back of a spoon. Strain through a fine sieve into a clean saucepan, season with cayenne, salt, and pepper, lift the flavor with a few drops of lemon juice, and set aside.

4 Coarsely chop the parsley leaves, place in an airtight container, and keep cool.

Finishing Touches

1 Drain the lentils, and reheat them with the butter. Season with salt and pepper, and stir in the parsley.

2 Reheat the cream sauce.

3 Season the langoustine tails with cayenne, salt, and pepper. Heat the clarified butter in a nonstick skillet until very hot, add the langoustine tails, and sauté for 30 seconds on each side. Immediately drain on paper towels.

Serves 4

12 langoustines
$1/2$ cup Puy lentils
Scant $1/2$ cup langoustine stock
   (page 196)
2 sprigs fresh rosemary
$3/4$ cup whipping cream
Ground cayenne pepper
Salt and freshly ground pepper
Lemon juice
2 sprigs Italian parsley
$1 1/2$ tablespoons unsalted butter
$1 1/2$ tablespoons clarified butter

Presentation
Arrange 3 langoustines on 4 warmed plates, with the tails facing outward. Spoon the lentils all around. Place a small spoonful of sauce between each langoustine, and garnish with a few leaves of the rosemary.

Pan-Fried Scallops with Belgian Endive and Lime

Serves 4

12 large scallops, in the shell
24 chive flowers on the stalk
  (optional)
1 lime
1 pound 2 ounces Belgian endives
1 ounce fresh ginger
1 large shallot
5$\frac{1}{2}$ tablespoons unsalted butter,
  softened
$\frac{1}{4}$ cup port
$\frac{1}{2}$ cup scallop ctock (page 197)
$\frac{1}{2}$ cup whipping cream
Salt and freshly ground pepper
Pinch of sugar
Juice of $\frac{1}{2}$ lemon
1$\frac{1}{2}$ tablespoons clarified butter

Preparation

1 Open the scallop shells. Wash them thoroughly under running water, remove the beards, and reserve the shells to make a scallop stock, if desired. Detach the scallops and corals.

2 If using, insert 2 chive flowers into the sides of each scallop, place the scallops on a plate, cover with plastic wrap, and refrigerate.

3 Blanch the corals for 2 minutes in boiling salted water, pat dry, and cut into $\frac{1}{8}$-inch dice. Place in an airtight container, and refrigerate.

4 Scrub the lime under hot water, and dry thoroughly. Peel off the zest with a swivel peeler. Using a small, very sharp knife, cut off the white pith that lies underneath the zest. Cut the zest into long, very fine julienne. Blanch for 2 minutes in boiling salted water, refresh in cold water, drain, and set aside. Juice the lime and reserve.

5 Discard the outer leaves of the Belgian endive. Cut the endives into whistle shapes by holding them with your left hand, and cutting them into scant $\frac{1}{2}$-inch chunks on the diagonal, giving them a quarter-turn after each cut. Pull the leaves apart, place in a plastic bag, seal well, and keep cool.

6 Peel and chop the ginger and shallot. Place in a small saucepan with $\frac{1}{2}$ tablespoon of the butter, and cook over medium heat until the shallot is translucent. Add the port and scallop stock, and reduce by half. Add the cream, and cook until the sauce is thick and creamy. Whisk in 3 tablespoons of the butter, strain the sauce through a fine sieve into a clean saucepan, and set aside.

Finishing Touches

1 Reheat the sauce, and season with salt, pepper, and a few drops of lime juice. Emulsify it with a hand blender, and stir in the scallop corals. Keep warm.

2 Scoop the Belgian endives into a salad bowl, season with sugar, salt, pepper, and 2 tablespoons of the lemon juice, and mix thoroughly with your hands.

3 Heat the remaining 2 tablespoons butter in a large, nonstick skillet, add the endive mixture, and stir over very high heat for no more than 3 minutes, so that they are cooked but not soft.

4 At the same time, season the scallops. Heat the clarified butter in a skillet until very hot, add the scallops, and pan-fry for 1 minute on each side, then immediately drain on paper towels.

Presentation
Place the endives in the center of the plates, and arrange 3 scallops on top. Pour the sauce around the endives, and scatter the lime zest over the top.

Grilled Scallops with Thyme, Pumpkin Cream, and Bacon "Frivolity"

Serves 4

²/₃ cup dried white haricot or great
   northern beans

12 large scallops, in the shell

¹/₂ onion, peeled and stuck with
   1 clove

1 bouquet garni (fresh thyme, parsley,
   and bay leaf)

Salt

Pumpkin Cream

1 onion

¹/₃ raw potato

5 ounces pumpkin flesh

1¹/₂ tablespoons unsalted butter

³/₄ cup scallop stock (page 197)

Scant ¹/₂ cup whipping cream

Pinch of ground nutmeg

Salt and freshly ground pepper

6 thin slices smoked bacon

1 orange

14 sprigs thyme

4 large black olives, pitted

1 anchovy fillet (optional)

5 tablespoons extra virgin olive oil

Ground cayenne pepper

Preparation

1 The day before you start the recipe, cover the haricot beans with cold water, and leave to soak in the refrigerator for at least 12 hours.

2 Open the scallop shells. Wash them thoroughly under running water, remove the beards, and reserve the shells to make a scallop stock if desired. Detach the scallops and corals. Place the scallops and corals on a plate, cover with plastic wrap, and refrigerate.

3 Blanch the corals for 2 minutes in boiling salted water, pat dry, and cut into ¹/₈-inch dice. Place in an airtight container, and refrigerate.

4 To make the haricot beans, rinse the soaked beans in plenty of cold water, and place in a saucepan with the ¹/₂ onion and bouquet garni, and cover with water. Bring to a boil, and cook until the beans are tender, making sure they remain covered with water; this will take 1¹/₂ to 2 hours, depending on the quality of the beans, and how long they have been soaking. Add salt three-fourths of the way through the cooking time. Remove from the heat and leave the beans in their cooking liquid.

5 To make the pumpkin cream, peel and finely chop the onion. Peel and thinly slice the potato. Cut the pumpkin flesh into ¹/₂-inch dice. Put the onion and butter in a saucepan, and cook over medium heat until the onion is translucent. Add the potato and pumpkin, pour in the scallop stock, bring to a boil, and cook for 10 minutes. Add the cream, boil for 2 minutes, and remove the pan from the heat. Season with nutmeg, salt, and pepper, press through a fine sieve into a clean saucepan, and set aside.

6 Preheat the oven to 275°F.

7 Halve the bacon slices lengthwise, place on a rimmed baking sheet, and cover with aluminum foil. Place another baking sheet on top to keep the bacon flat. Cook in the oven for 20 minutes, and set aside.

8 Scrub the orange under hot water, dry thoroughly, and grate 1 teaspoon of zest.

9 Pick off the leaves from 2 thyme sprigs, and chop finely. Chop the olives and the anchovy fillet, if using. Mix with the olive oil, add the grated orange zest, and set aside.

Finishing Touches

1 Heat a grill or griddle pan.

2 Drain the beans, add them to the pumpkin cream, and reheat.

3 Season the scallops with cayenne, salt, and pepper, and grill for 1 minute on each side. Immediately drain on paper towels.

4 Brush the scallops with the olive oil mixture, and scatter on the diced corals.

Presentation
Pour the pumpkin cream and beans over 4 warmed plates. Place 3 scallops on top, and stick 2 lengths of bacon vertically into each scallop. Place a few sprigs of thyme in the center.

Pan-Fried Langoustines with
Flageolets and Lemon Emulsion

Serves 4 (as a main course; for an appetizer, use smaller langoustines, and reduce the quantity of flageolets by one-third)

12 giant langoustines

2¼ pounds fresh flageolets, in the pod, or 10 ounces fresh shell beans

1 green onion

½ clove garlic

3 tablespoons unsalted butter

Salt and freshly ground pepper

2 tomatoes

¾ cup vegetable bouillon (page 194)

Juice of ½ lemon

2 sprigs tarragon

½ cup plus 1 tablespoon extra virgin olive oil

Guérande *fleur de sel*

Coarsely crushed black peppercorns

Preparation

1   Remove the langoustine heads, and shell the tails, leaving the last two rings of the shell attached. Place on a plate, cover with plastic wrap, and refrigerate.

2   Shell the beans and cook for 7 to 8 minutes in boiling salted water. Refresh in cold water, and drain.

3   Peel the onion and garlic, and chop very finely. Place in a saucepan with the butter, and cook gently until the onion is translucent. Add the flageolets, season, and set aside.

4   Cut a cross in the bases of the tomatoes, drop them into boiling water for 15 seconds, then immediately plunge them into cold water. Peel, seed, and cut into ¼-inch dice. Place in an airtight container, and keep cool.

5   Reduce the vegetable bouillon by half, add the lemon juice, and set aside.

6   Pull off the tarragon leaves, chop finely, place in an airtight container, and keep cool.

Finishing Touches

1   Reheat the flageolets with 2 tablespoons of the reduced bouillon and a drizzle of the olive oil. Season.

2   Reheat the remaining reduced bouillon, and whisk in a scant ½ cup of the olive oil with a hand blender to emulsify. Stir in the tomatoes and tarragon, and adjust the seasoning.

3   Lightly season the langoustines. Heat 1 tablespoon of the olive oil in a skillet until very hot, put in the langoustines, and pan-fry for 50 seconds on each side. Immediately drain on paper towels.

Presentation
Place the flageolets in the center of 4 warmed plates, and place 2 langoustines on top, with the tails facing outward. Coat the langoustines very lightly with the lemon emulsion, and sprinkle a few flakes of *fleur de sel* and a little crushed pepper over the top.

Poultry, Rabbit, and Feathered Game

Pink Roast Duck with Châteauneuf du Pape, Celeriac, and Braised Lettuce and Carrot Wheels

Serves 4

2 ducks, 5 pounds each
1 celeriac (celery root)
Juice of 1 lemon
1 teaspoon unsalted butter, softened,
   plus extra for greasing

Châteauneuf Sauce

1 shallot
3 tablespoons unsalted butter
1 clove garlic, peeled and crushed
1 sprig thyme
1½ cups Châteauneuf du Pape
Scant ½ cup brown veal stock
   (page 197)
Scant ½ cup chicken stock (page 194)

Braised Lettuce

1 large romaine lettuce
2 carrots
1 onion
2 tablespoons unsalted butter, plus
   more for dotting
¾ cup chicken stock (page 194)

1 tablespoon grapeseed oil
1 tablespoon clarified butter
Salt and freshly ground pepper
Fresh herbs, for garnish

Preparation

1   If necessary, singe the ducks, cut off the wingtips and necks, and remove the oil gland situated under the parson's nose. Empty the cavities, and truss the ducks. Brush with butter, place on a plate, cover with plastic wrap, and refrigerate.

2   Peel the celeriac, and cut it into ½-inch-thick slices. Using a 2-inch fluted pastry cutter, cut the celeriac into 12 disks. Bring a saucepan of salted water to a boil, acidulate with the lemon juice, add the celeriac and ½ teaspoon of the butter, and cook for about 5 minutes, until a knife blade pierces the celeriac disks easily. Drain and set aside.

3   To make the sauce, peel and finely chop the shallot, place in a saucepan with 2 teaspoons of the butter, the garlic, and thyme, and cook until translucent. Add the wine, veal stock, and chicken stock, bring to a boil, and reduce by three-fourths, until only about ⅔ cup of liquid remains. Set aside.

4   To make the braised lettuce, blanch the lettuce in boiling salted water for 5 minutes, refresh in cold water, and drain. Peel the carrots and onion, slice them finely, and cook in a saucepan with the butter for 5 minutes. Cover with the chicken stock, and cook gently until very soft. Spread the drained lettuce on a cloth, making sure that the larger leaves lie flat, and that the thickness is even throughout. Cover with the carrot and onion mixture. Make two light marks with a knife, the first 2 inches below the top of the lettuce leaves, and the second 2½ inches below the first. Fold the lettuce down, and up, at the marks, then form into a flattish roll. Cut into 1-inch rounds, arrange them on a baking sheet, dot with flakes of butter, and set aside.

Cooking

1   Preheat the oven to 475°F.

2   Heat the oil in a roasting pan until very hot, place the ducks in the pan, laying them on one thigh, and sear for 2 minutes. Turn onto the other thigh, and sear for another 2 minutes. This will release the fat.

3   Immediately place the roasting pan in the very hot oven, and roast the ducks for 8 minutes on one thigh, then 8 minutes on the other thigh, and finally, on their backs for 4 minutes (20 minutes total).

4   Remove the ducks from the oven, pour off the juices and fat from inside the cavities, and lay the ducks breast-side down, with the parson's nose slightly elevated. Cover tightly with aluminum foil, and leave to rest for 10 minutes.

Finishing Touches

1   Decrease the oven temperature to 350°F.

2   Place the baking sheet containing the lettuce rounds in the oven, and heat for 6 to 8 minutes.

3   Fry the celeriac discs in the clarified butter until golden brown, and season.

4   Reheat the sauce, whisk in 2½ tablespoons of the butter, and season.

Free-Range Chicken Breasts with Cucumber and Orange Zest

Serves 4

2 free-range chickens, with their livers
    and hearts, 2³/₄ pounds each
1 shallot
2 sprigs Italian parsley
5 tablespoons unsalted butter,
    softened
Salt and freshly ground pepper
1 orange
1 large cucumber
¹/₂ red bell pepper
¹/₂ yellow bell pepper
2-inch piece fresh ginger
1 tablespoon clarified butter
Scant ³/₄ cup brown chicken stock
    (page 198)
4 tablespoons port
Fresh lemon juice
¹/₄ cup chicken stock (page 194)
1 tablespoon snipped fresh dill

Preparation

1   Cut off the chicken breasts, leaving the wing bones attached, but scraping off
    their flesh. Keep the legs for another use.

2   Peel and finely chop the shallot. Chop the parsley.

3   Finely slice the chicken livers and hearts. Heat 2 teaspoons of the butter in a
    skillet over high heat, and quickly sauté the livers, hearts, and chopped shallot.
    Remove from the heat, and stir in the parsley. Let cool.

4   Make an incision in the thickest part of the chicken breasts, between the fillets,
    and stuff with the liver and heart mixture. Brush the breasts with 4 teaspoons
    of the butter, season with salt and pepper, wrap them separately in plastic wrap,
    and refrigerate.

5   Scrub the orange under hot water, pat dry, and grate 1 tablespoon of zest. Place in
    a small airtight container, and keep cool.

6   Peel the cucumber, quarter it lengthwise, remove the seeds and cut the flesh into
    thin, 1¹/₂-inch-long strips. Blanch in boiling salted water for 2 minutes, refresh in
    cold water, and drain. Set aside.

7   Peel the bell peppers with a swivel peeler, halve, remove the seed and white ribs,
    and cut into ¹/₈-inch dice. Blanch for 3 to 4 minutes in boiling salted water,
    refresh in cold water, and drain. Set aside.

8   Peel the ginger, and cut into the finest possible julienne. Heat the clarified butter
    until very hot, add the ginger julienne, and fry briefly, then drain on paper
    towels. Set aside.

9   Pour the brown chicken stock and the port into a small saucepan, reduce to a
    scant ¹/₂ cup, and add a few drops of lemon juice. Set aside.

Finishing Touches

1   Leaving them wrapped in the plastic wrap, steam the chicken breasts for
    10 minutes.

2   Reheat the stock and port reduction.

3   Unwrap the chicken breasts, place in a skillet, and set over medium heat. Baste
    them several times with a little of the stock and port reduction, until well glazed.
    Keep warm.

4   Dilute the remaining reduction with 1 or 2 tablespoons of the chicken stock,
    then refine the sauce by whisking in 4 teaspoons butter, and adjust the seasoning.

5   At the same time, put the peppers and cucumber in a shallow pan with 2 or
    3 tablespoons of the chicken stock and the remaining 2 tablespoons butter, and
    cook over high heat until the vegetables are soft and the butter has emulsified.
    Add the orange zest and dill, and season.

Presentation
Slice each chicken breast on the diagonal into 5 thick
slices. Arrange on warmed plates, surround with
vegetables, pour the sauce around, and scatter ginger
julienne over the top.

Epigrams of Pigeon Breast with Bacon-Stuffed Cabbage

Preparation

1 Cut off the pigeon breasts, and discard the skin. Cut off the legs, with as much skin as possible, bone them cut through the end, without slicing along the bone and leaving on the tips of the leg bones.

2 Cut the foie gras into small batons.

3 Make an incision in the breasts, and place a few batons of foie gras inside. Close up the breasts, pressing them together lightly. Reserve the remaining foie gras.

4 Reserve 4 sprigs of the parsley for the garnish. Chop the remaining leaves very finely, and mix them with the bread crumbs.

5 Break the egg into a shallow bowl, and beat lightly. Place the bread crumbs and flour into two other bowls. Season the pigeon breasts with salt and pepper, and coat them first in the flour, then in the egg, and finally in the bread crumbs. Place on a plate, cover with plastic wrap, and refrigerate.

6 To make the forcemeat, cut the pigeon livers and hearts into $1/4$-inch dice. Peel and finely chop the shallot. Clean the mushrooms, and chop them. Heat $1 1/2$ tablespoons of the butter in a small skillet, add all the forcemeat ingredients, and sauté. Season and let cool, then mix in the reserved foie gras. Chop a couple of times with a knife to mix the stuffing.

7 Stuff the thighs with the forcemeat, fold the skin over to close, and secure with toothpicks. Place on a plate, cover with plastic wrap, and refrigerate.

8 To make the sauce, chop the pigeon carcasses. Heat the oil in a shallow pan until very hot, add the carcasses, and quickly brown them, stirring. Remove them from the pan, and press to extract all the juices. Reserve the juices.

9 Return the carcasses to the pan, add the mirepoix, and brown over high heat for 5 minutes. Deglaze with the wine and Madeira, add the chicken stock and reduce for 10 minutes. Strain through a fine sieve into a small saucepan, and set aside.

10 To make the bacon-stuffed cabbage, remove the cabbage leaves, and blanch in plenty of boiling salted water, taking care that they do not fall apart. Refresh, choose the 8 best leaves, cut out the thick central ribs, and lay the leaves flat on a cloth to dry.

11 Remove the large ribs from the remaining cabbage leaves, cut the leaves into approximately $1 1/4$-inch squares, and drain. Remove the bacon rinds, if necessary, and cut into $1/8$-inch-wide lardons. Peel and finely chop the onion, place in a wide shallow pan or skillet with 4 teaspoons of the butter, and cook over medium heat until translucent. Add the lardons, and cook until they have rendered their fat, but do not brown them. Stir in the squares of cabbage, moisten with a few drops of water, and cook for about 5 minutes, until the cabbage is tender. Season, and stir in the remaining 2 tablespoons butter.

12 Season the reserved cabbage leaves, place some of the bacon stuffing on each leaf, and form into a ball. Arrange on a buttered baking sheet, and put a flake of butter on top of each cabbage ball. Set aside.

Serves 4 (depending on the importance of the meal and the number of courses, half a pigeon per person may be ample)

2 to 4 plump Bresse pigeons, about 1 pound each, singed and cleaned if necessary, livers and hearts reserved

$1 1/2$ ounces terrine of foie gras

1 cup fresh Italian parsley

1 cup fresh white bread crumbs

1 egg

2 tablespoons all-purpose flour

Salt and freshly ground pepper

1 shallot

5 ounces chanterelles

$2 1/2$ tablespoons unsalted butter

1 tablespoon grapeseed oil

$1/2$ cup mirepoix (mixed carrot, onion, and celery, cut into $1/4$-inch dice)

2 tablespoons white wine

1 tablespoon Madeira

Scant $3/4$ cup chicken stock (page 194)

Bacon-Stuffed Cabbage

1 savoy cabbage, cored

7 ounces smoked bacon, sliced $1/8$-inch thick

1 onion

$3 1/2$ tablespoons unsalted butter

2 tablespoons clarified butter

continued

▼

Finishing Touches

1 Preheat the oven to 350°F.

2 Place the baking sheet in the hot oven, and bake the stuffed cabbage for 7 to 8 minutes.

3 Season the pigeon breasts and legs, and sauté in the clarified butter for 6 to 8 minutes.

4 Reheat the sauce, and whisk the remaining 1 tablespoon of butter and the juices from the pigeon bones. Season.

Presentation
Place 2 pigeon breasts, 2 thighs, and 2 stuffed cabbage leaves on each warmed plate. Coat lightly with sauce, and serve the rest of the sauce on the side. Garnish with the reserved parsley sprigs.

Roast Partridge with Aromatic Herbs and Celeriac Jus

Preparation

1 Place 1 teaspoon of the butter, ¹/₂ sprig of thyme, and ¹/₄ bay leaf inside each partridge, smear the birds with butter, then place on a plate, cover with plastic wrap, and refrigerate.

2 If you wish, keep the livers for roasting separately. Clean the hearts, gizzards, necks, and wings, and dice them all. Mix them into the mirepoix, add a bay leaf and a sprig of thyme, cut into pieces, and place in the refrigerator.

3 To make the celeriac jus, peel the celeriac, cut into ¹/₂-inch slices, then into ¹/₂-inch cubes. Melt the butter in a deep skillet and fry the celeriac gently until pale golden all over. Half cover with veal stock, season with salt and continue to cook gently, stirring with a wooden spoon, to coat and glaze the celeriac. Do not overcook it; it should be al dente. Set aside.

Finishing Touches and Cooking

1 Preheat the oven to 475°F.

2 Mix 2 tablespoons of fine salt with the four-spice powder and season the partridges inside and out with this mixture.

3 Heat 1¹/₂ tablespoons of the butter in a wide, ovenproof casserole until foaming. Add the partridges, laying them on one thigh. Roast in the oven for 5 minutes, then turn the birds onto the other thigh, taking care not to pierce the flesh. Add the mirepoix mixture, and return the casserole to the oven for 5 minutes. Open the oven door, add 4 tablespoons of the butter, turn the partridges onto their backs, and roast for 4 minutes longer, basting constantly.

4 Put the partridges in a fairly deep baking dish, laying them breast-side down with their feet resting on the edge of the dish so that the breast will remain moist. Cover with aluminum foil and leave to rest on the open oven door while you finish the dish.

5 Gently reheat the celeriac jus, stirring occasionally.

6 Pour off the fat and deglaze the pan with ¹/₄ cup water and let it reduce completely. Add the remaining veal stock, simmer gently for 2 minutes, then strain the jus through a fine sieve into a small saucepan and whisk in 1¹/₂ tablespoons butter. Check and adjust the seasoning.

7 Carve off the partridge breasts and legs.

Serves 4

¹/₂ cup unsalted butter
6 sprigs thyme
1¹/₂ fresh bay leaves
2 partridges, plucked and drawn, if necessary, and trussed (offal, wings, and neck reserved)
1 cup mirepoix (mixed carrot, onion, and celery, cut into ¹/₄-inch dice)
Fine salt and freshly ground pepper

Celeriac Jus
1 celeriac (celery root)
1¹/₂ tablespoons unsalted butter
¹/₂ to ³/₄ cup brown veal stock (page 197)

1 tablespoon four-spice powder (cloves, ginger, white pepper, nutmeg)
4 sprigs fresh Italian parsley, for garnish

Presentation
Place 1 partridge thigh in the center of each warmed plate and place a breast on top. Spoon some diced celeriac and a touch of jus around the edge. Decorate with a sprig each of thyme and parsley.

111

Confit Duckling with Spices and Lime

Serves 4

2 ducklings, 3 pounds each

$^1/_3$ cup honey

$^1/_3$ cup Dijon mustard

1 level tablespoon four-spice powder
(cloves, ginger, white pepper, and
nutmeg)

2 limes

1 cup mirepoix (mixed carrot, onion,
and celery, cut into $^1/_4$-inch dice)

2 lemons

1 orange

2 cloves garlic

1 sprig thyme

4 sprigs parsley

2 tablespoons grapeseed oil

Salt and freshly ground pepper

$^3/_4$ cup chicken stock (page 194)

$^3/_4$ cup brown veal stock (page 197)

$^1/_4$ cup unsalted butter

Presentation

Sprinkle the blanched lemon zest julienne, or substitute 2 tablespoons finely snipped chives over the ducklings and place the peeled segments around. Serve the sauce in a sauceboat. Accompany the dish with French beans, braised lettuce, buttered spinach, or what you will.

Carving

Return the ducklings to the kitchen, carve off the breasts, and serve them first with the garnishes. Return the carcasses with the legs to the oven for about 10 minutes. Carve off the legs, and serve as a second helping, with a salad.

Preparation

1 Singe the ducklings, if necessary, and empty the cavities. Remove the oil gland situated under the parson's nose, and truss the ducklings.

2 Mix the honey, mustard, and four-spice powder.

3 Halve one of the limes, and rub it over the skin of the ducklings. Squeeze the lime halves, and pour the juice into the cavities.

4 Brush the ducklings four times with the honey and spice mixture, at one-hour intervals, then leave in a cool place overnight.

5 Chop the giblets, excluding the livers and hearts (which will not be used in this recipe), and mix them with the mirepoix.

6 Scrub the remaining lime, the 2 lemons, and the orange under hot water, and dry thoroughly.

7 Using a swivel peeler, thinly pare the zest of one of the lemons, the remaining lime, and one-third of the orange zest. Set aside.

8 Squeeze the juice of all the citrus fruits, place in a sealed container, and reserve for making the sauce.

9 Peel the garlic, halve the cloves lengthwise, and remove the green germ. Blanch the cloves for 2 minutes in boiling salted water. Refresh in cold water and drain.

10 Pick off the thyme and parsley leaves.

11 Finely chop the herbs, garlic, and citrus zests, and mix together. Place in an airtight container, and keep cool.

12 Peel the second lemon with a swivel peeler carefully, removing all the white pith from the strips of zest, and cut the zest into the finest possible julienne. Blanch in boiling water for 30 seconds, refresh in cold water, drain, and reserve for the garnish.

13 Peel off all the remaining pith from the lemon, and cut the fruit into segments between membranes, discarding the membrane. Place in an airtight container, and keep cool.

Finishing Touches and Cooking

1 Put the oil in a roasting pan, place in the oven, and heat the oven to 500°F.

2 Season the ducklings inside and out with salt and pepper.

3 When the oven is very hot, lay the ducklings on one thigh in the roasting pan, and roast for 10 minutes. Turn them onto the other thigh, and roast for 10 minutes longer. Put the mirepoix mixture around the ducklings, turn them onto their backs, and roast for 10 minutes.

4 Remove the roasting pan from the oven, and transfer the ducklings to a platter.

5 Reduce the oven temperature to 350°F.

6 Pour off the fat from the roasting pan, place it over high heat, and let the pan juices scorch just slightly on the bottom. Deglaze with the citrus juices, reduce by half, then add the chicken stock and the veal stock. Remove the roasting pan from the heat.

7 Return the ducklings to the roasting pan, return the pan to the oven, and roast for 30 minutes, basting frequently with the pan juices to make them shiny and glazed.

8 Remove from the oven, and place the ducklings on a warmed platter.

9 Set the roasting pan over high heat, deglaze with $^1/_4$ cup water, scraping up the juices from the bottom of the pan, bring up to a simmer, adjust the seasoning, then strain the juice through a fine sieve into a warmed sauceboat.

10 Heat the butter in a small skillet, add the garlic-zest mixture, and brown for 1 minute. Remove from the heat, and pour over the ducklings.

Vinegar-Glazed Pigeons with Potato Gâteaux

Serves 4

4 plump Bresse pigeons, about
 1 pound each, singed and cleaned,
 if necessary, giblets reserved
2 to 3 tablespoons unsalted butter,
 softened

Potato Gâteaux
$^1/_2$ cup clarified butter
13 ounces salad-style (not floury)
 potatoes
Salt and freshly ground pepper
2 teaspoons unsalted butter, melted

2 tablespoons grapeseed oil
1 cup mirepoix (mixed carrot, onion,
 and celery, cut into $^1/_4$-inch dice)
$^1/_4$ cup balsamic vinegar
2 tablespoons sherry vinegar
$^1/_4$ cup port
$^1/_4$ cup chicken stock (page 194)
$^5/_8$ cup brown chicken stock
 (page 198)
Fresh herbs, for garnish

Preparation

1 Brush the pigeons with butter, place on a plate, cover with plastic wrap, and refrigerate.

2 Dice the giblets, excluding the livers and hearts (which will not be used in this recipe).

3 To make the potato gâteaux, brush four tartlet pans, 2 to $2^1/_2$ inches in diameter and $1^1/_2$ inches deep, with the clarified butter. Peel the potatoes, cut them into circles, and slice very thinly, using a mandoline or food processor. Pat dry in a cloth, mix with the remaining clarified butter, and season with salt and pepper.

4 Line the tartlet pans with the potato slices, starting on the base, then the sides, overlapping them evenly. Fill up the pans with the potatoes, brush the surface with a little whole butter, place on a plate, cover with plastic wrap, and keep cool.

Finishing Touches and Cooking

1 Put the oil in a deep, ovenproof skillet or a flame-proof baking dish, place in the oven, and preheat to 475°F.

2 Season the pigeons inside and out with salt and pepper.

3 When the oven is hot, lay the pigeons on one thigh in the skillet, and roast for 7 minutes. Turn them onto the other thigh, add the mirepoix and the giblets, and roast for 7 minutes longer. Remove the skillet from the oven, and transfer the pigeons to a platter. Pour off the fat from the skillet, set it over high heat, and deglaze with the two vinegars and the port, scraping up the juices. Quickly pour in the two chicken stocks, decrease the heat, and gently reduce the sauce by half. Return the pigeons to the skillet, laying them on their backs. Return to the oven, leaving the door open, and cook for a final 5 minutes, basting continuously with the cooking juices to glaze the birds.

4 Remove the pigeons, and place them breast-side down in a deep dish with the parson's nose elevated. Cover with aluminum foil, and keep warm while you cook the potato gâteaux.

5 Put the tartlet pans on a baking sheet, and cook in the hot oven for 6 minutes. Unmold the gâteaux, place them directly on the baking sheet, and return to the oven for 12 minutes.

6 To make the jus, strain the pigeon cooking juices into a small saucepan, set over medium heat, and simmer until syrupy. Adjust the seasoning, and, if necessary, thicken by whisking in 4 teaspoons of the remaining butter.

Presentation
Halve the pigeons, and garnish with small bunches of
fresh herbs. Place the potato gâteaux beside them,
and accompany with a buttered green vegetable.
Serve the jus separately in a sauceboat.

Roast Guinea Fowl with Indian Spices, Deep-Fried Herbs, and Basmati Rice Pilaf

Preparation

1 Rub the guinea fowl with a little of the curry powder. Cut the necks and wings into $^3/_4$-inch pieces, dust them with curry powder, and mix with the mirepoix. Put everything onto plates, cover with plastic wrap, and refrigerate.

2 Discard the green part of the leek and the outer leaves. Halve the white part lengthwise, then cut it into $2^1/_2$-inch lengths. Lay these flat on the work surface, and cut into very fine julienne. Place in an airtight container, and keep cool.

3 Peel the eggplant, cut it lengthwise into $^1/_8$-inch-wide strips, then into $^1/_2$-inch diamonds. Do the same with the zucchini. Peel the bell peppers with a swivel peeler, open them up, remove the seeds and white ribs, and cut into $^1/_2$-inch diamonds. Put all of the vegetables in an airtight container, and keep cool.

4 Prepare the curry sauce as on page 62.

Cooking

1 Put the oil in a shallow ovenproof skillet or a flame-proof baking dish, place in the oven, and preheat to 475°F.

2 Season the guinea fowl inside and out with salt and pepper.

3 When the oven is hot, lay the guinea fowl in the skillet on one thigh, and roast for 8 minutes. Turn onto the other thigh, and roast for another 8 minutes. Turn over onto their backs, add the butter, leave the oven door open, and cook for a final 4 minutes, basting the birds continuously with the foaming butter. Remove from the oven, and lower the temperature to 350°F.

4 Transfer the guinea fowl to an ovenproof dish, laying them breast-side down, with their feet resting on the edge of the dish, so that the juices run down into the breasts and keep them moist. Cover with aluminum foil, and leave to rest.

5 Pour off the fat from the skillet, and place over high heat until the juices scorch just slightly on the bottom, then deglaze with a scant $^1/_2$ cup water, scraping up the juices, and remove from the heat.

6 Pour the deglazed juices into the saucepan with the curry sauce, set over medium heat, and simmer for 10 minutes.

7 To make the pilaf, heat the oven to 350°F. Bring the chicken stock to a boil. Peel and finely chop the onion, place in a saucepan with the oil, and cook over medium heat until translucent. Add the rice, and stir with a wooden spoon until it, too, is translucent. Pour in the boiling stock and immediately bring back to a boil. Cover, and cook in the hot oven for 12 minutes. Remove from the oven, season with salt, dot with flakes of the butter, and fluff the rice with a fork to separate the grains. Keep warm.

8 To cook the vegetables, dust the eggplant and zucchini diamonds with flour, and coat lightly with cream. Heat half of the clarified butter in a skillet until very hot, and quickly sauté the diamonds just until golden brown. Season.

9 Coat the bell pepper diamonds with flour and cream in the same way, and sauté them separately in the remaining, very hot clarified butter. Season, and mix with the eggplant and zucchini.

10 Heat the deep-frying oil to 300°F, deep-fry the basil and parsley, and drain on paper towels.

11 Carve the guinea fowl.

Serves 4

2 guinea fowl, $2^3/_4$ pounds each, cleaned and trussed (necks and wings reserved)

2 teaspoons Madras curry powder

$^1/_2$ cup mirepoix (mixed carrot, onion, and celery, cut into $^1/_4$-inch dice)

1 leek

1 eggplant

1 zucchini

$^1/_2$ red bell pepper

$^1/_2$ yellow bell pepper

Scant $^3/_4$ cup curry sauce (page 62)

2 tablespoons grapeseed oil

Salt and freshly ground pepper

2 tablespoons unsalted butter

Basmati Rice Pilaf

$1^3/_4$ cups chicken stock (page 194)

1 small onion

3 tablespoons grapeseed oil

$1^1/_4$ cups basmati rice, well rinsed

2 tablespoons unsalted butter

3 tablespoons all-purpose flour

3 tablespoons whipping cream

$^1/_4$ cup clarified butter

4 large fresh basil leaves

Leaves from a sprig of curly parsley

Leaves from a sprig of Italian parsley

Oil, for deep-frying

Presentation
Put some of the pilaf into the center of warmed plates, place a guinea fowl breast on top, and scatter the vegetable mixture over it. Surround with a ribbon of sauce, and serve the rest of the sauce separately. Scatter the deep-fried herbs over the top. Serve the guinea fowl thighs as a second helping, with a salad.

115

Roast Guinea Fowl with Spring Vegetables and Fresh Morel Mushrooms

Serves 4

4 guinea fowl, 1 pound 2 ounces
  each, cleaned and trussed (livers
  reserved, necks and wings
  chopped)

Salt and freshly ground pepper

1 sprig rosemary

2 sprigs thyme

$^1/_3$ cup unsalted butter, softened

10 ounces fresh morel mushrooms

1 tablespoon wine vinegar

1 shallot

12 baby carrots

1 zucchini

2 cups chanterelle mushrooms,
  cleaned

2 tablespoons grapeseed oil

Scant $^1/_2$ cup chicken stock
  (page 194)

1 tablespoon Madeira

$^1/_4$ cup whipping cream

Sprigs of curly parsley, for garnish

Preparation

1 Place a liver inside each guinea fowl, season the cavities with salt and pepper, and place a 1$^1/_4$-inch piece of rosemary and $^1/_2$ sprig of thyme inside each. Truss the birds, brush them with butter, place on a plate, cover with plastic wrap, and refrigerate.

2 Cut off and discard the sandy, dirty stems of the morels. Halve the morels lengthwise, and wash quickly in a bowl of water acidulated with the vinegar. Drain, and keep washing the morels briefly in water, this time without vinegar, to eliminate all the sand and dirt. Drain, and place in a covered container lined with a folded cloth.

3 Peel and finely chop the shallot, place in an airtight container, and keep cool.

4 Peel and slice the carrots and cook in boiling salted water for 3 to 4 minutes; they should still be slightly crisp. Drain, and set aside.

5 Cut the zucchini lengthwise into $^1/_4$-inch strips. Blanch for 1 minute in boiling salted water, refresh in cold water. Set aside.

6 Slice the chanterelles. In a nonstick skillet, sauté until they give up all their liquid. Season and set aside.

Finishing Touches

1 Put the oil in a deep ovenproof skillet or a flame-proof baking dish, place in the oven, and preheat to 475°F.

2 When the oven is hot, lay the guinea fowl on one thigh in the skillet, surround them with the chopped necks and wings, and roast for 6 minutes. Turn them onto the other thigh, baste, and roast for 6 minutes longer. Turn the birds onto their backs, add 2 tablespoons of the butter, leave the oven door open, and roast for a final 6 minutes, basting frequently with the foaming butter.

3 Remove the skillet, and turn off the oven. Transfer the guinea fowl to a deep dish, laying them breast-side down, with their feet resting on the edge of the dish, so that the juices run down into the breasts and keep them moist. Cover with aluminum foil, and leave to rest on the open oven door.

4 Pour off the fat from the skillet, set it over high heat, and deglaze with the stock and 3 tablespoons of water, scraping up the flavorful crust. Reduce to about 3 good tablespoons of juice, strain through a fine sieve into a bowl, and season.

5 Heat a nonstick skillet over high heat until very hot. Add the morels, season with salt, and stir until they render out their liquid. As soon as it has evaporated, add the chopped shallot and 1 tablespoon of the butter, and stir for 30 seconds. Add the Madeira, let it evaporate, then add the guinea fowl juices and the cream, and cook over medium heat until the sauce comes together. Adjust the seasoning.

6 At the same time, heat 4 teaspoons of the butter in a nonstick skillet, add the carrots, zucchini, and chanterelles, and stir until heated through. Season with salt.

7 Cut the guinea fowl in half.

Presentation
Place the 2 halves of guinea fowl in the center of each warmed plate, put the morels at the top, and the mixture of vegetables on each side. Garnish with parsley.

Black Chicken with Puy Lentils and Thyme Cream

Serves 4

1 small bunch thyme

1 oven-ready free-range black
   chicken, about 3¼ pounds

⅓ cup unsalted butter, softened

2¼ cups Puy lentils (see Sauté of
   Duck Foie Gras with Lentils,
   page 57)

2 tablespoons grapeseed oil

Salt and freshly ground pepper

1 cup mirepoix (mixed carrot, onion,
   and celery, cut into ¼-inch dice)

¼ cup white wine

Scant ½ cup chicken stock
   (page 194)

Scant ½ cup heavy cream

1 tablespoon gin

White wine vinegar

4 sprigs Italian parsley, for garnish

Preparation

1 Place 1 sprig of the thyme inside the chicken. Brush the skin with a little butter, place the bird on a plate, cover with plastic wrap, and refrigerate.

2 Cook the lentils, following the recipe on page 57, doubling the quantities, and including the bacon. Reserve them in the cooking liquid.

3 Pick off enough thyme leaves to make 1 heaping tablespoon, and set aside.

Cooking

1 Put the oil in a roasting pan or a flame-proof baking dish, place in the oven, and preheat to 450°F.

2 Season the chicken inside and out with salt and pepper.

3 When the oven is hot, lay the chicken on one thigh in the roasting pan, and roast for 15 minutes. Turn onto the other thigh, surround with the mirepoix, and roast for 15 minutes longer. Turn the chicken onto its back, add 2 tablespoons of the butter, and roast for a final 10 minutes, basting frequently with the foaming butter.

4 Remove the roasting pan, and turn off the oven. Put the chicken breast-side down in a deep dish with the feet elevated and resting on the edge so that the juices run down into the breast. Cover with aluminum foil, and leave to rest on the open oven door.

5 Pour off the fat from the roasting pan, set it over high heat, and deglaze with the wine and 3 tablespoons of water, scraping up the crust with a wooden spoon. Add the chicken stock, and reduce by half. Add the cream, and reduce until the sauce is thick enough to coat the spoon. Strain through a fine sieve into a small saucepan, and add 1 heaping teaspoon of the thyme leaves. Set over low heat, whisk in 2 tablespoons of the butter, season, and "lift" the sauce with the gin. Bring just to a simmer, and remove the pan from the heat.

6 Stir a few drops of vinegar into the lentils, reheat them, adjust the seasoning, and drain.

Presentation
Spread the lentils over a warmed serving platter, put the chicken on top, and coat with some of the sauce. Serve the rest of the sauce separately. Garnish with sprigs of thyme and Italian parsley.

Saddle of Rabbit with North African Spices and Swiss Chard Gâteaux

Serves 4

2 saddles of rabbit

1 tablespoon extra virgin olive oil

2 sprigs thyme

1 tablespoon *ras-el-hanout* (North African spice mixture)

1 small clove garlic, peeled

1 bay leaf

Swiss Chard Gâteaux

2¹/₂ tablespoons unsalted butter, softened

12 sheets of phyllo

1 pound 2 ounces young Swiss chard, well washed

Juice of ¹/₂ lemon

1 green onion

Scant ¹/₂ cup whipping cream

Salt and freshly ground pepper

Ground nutmeg

2 tablespoons grapeseed oil

2 tablespoons unsalted butter

Scant ¹/₂ cup chicken stock (page 194)

¹/₄ cup whipping cream

1 tablespoon crushed pink peppercorns, for garnish

4 sprigs cilantro, for garnish

Preparation

1 Trim off all the small pieces of skin and sinews from the saddles of rabbit. Make a cut all along their length on either side of the backbone, leaving 1¹/₄ inches uncut at each end. Reserve all the trimmings.

2 Brush the saddles with olive oil. Pick off the leaves from 1 sprig of the thyme, and rub them over the saddles. Dice the rabbit trimmings, and mix them with a small pinch of the *ras-el-hanout,* the garlic, the remaining 1 sprig thyme, and the bay leaf. Place everything on a plate, cover with plastic wrap, and refrigerate.

3 Preheat the oven to 425°F.

4 To make the Swiss chard gâteaux, lightly butter 4 tartlet pans, about 3 inches in diameter. Brush the sheets of phyllo with butter, and stack them in 4 piles of 3 sheets each. Cut out 4 circles with a large pastry cutter, and line the tartlet pans with the phyllo circles. Cover with a second tart pan to keep the phyllo in place, and press down.

5 Bake the tarts in the oven for 4 minutes, remove the top pans, and continue to bake until the phyllo bases are golden brown. Remove from the oven, and set aside.

6 Separate the chard leaves from the ribs. Cook the leaves in boiling salted water for 3 minutes, refresh in cold water, and drain. Cut into ¹/₂-inch-wide strips.

7 Peel the ribs, cut into ¹/₄-inch slices, and cook in boiling water acidulated with the lemon juice, for 5 to 6 minutes. Refresh in cold water, and drain.

8 Peel and finely chop the green onion, and place in a saucepan with 4 teaspoons of the butter. Add the chard ribs, then the leaves, and cook for 1 minute, stirring. Add the cream, and cook until thickened. Season with salt, pepper, and nutmeg, and set aside.

Finishing Touches and Cooking

1 Put the grapeseed oil in a roasting pan, place in the oven, and preheat to 350°F.

2 Season the saddles of rabbit with salt and the remaining *ras-el-hanout.*

3 When the oven is hot, put the rabbit in the roasting pan, resting on one fillet. Surround with the diced rabbit trimmings mixture, and roast for 4 minutes. Turn the saddles so that the other fillet is resting against the roasting pan, roast for 4 minutes, then place the fillets flat on the bones. Add the butter, leave the oven door open, and roast for 4 minutes longer, basting the rabbit continuously with the foaming butter. Invert the saddles onto a plate, cover with aluminum foil, and leave to rest in a warm place.

4 Increase the oven temperature to 475°F.

5 Pour off the fat from the roasting pan, and deglaze with the chicken stock, scraping up the crust. Strain the juices through a sieve into a small saucepan, add the cream, and simmer for 5 minutes. Season, and keep warm.

6 Fill the phyllo cases with the creamy chard, and place in the hot oven for 3 minutes to heat through.

7 Carve off the rabbit fillets, and slice into thin strips.

Presentation
Fan out the rabbit strips on warmed plates, drizzle with some of the sauce, and sprinkle with the crushed pink peppercorns. Place a Swiss chard gâteau to one side. Garnish with a sprig of cilantro.

Meat and
Furred Game

Roast Rack of Venison with Fresh Green Peppercorns

Serves 4

2 racks of venison, 1¼ pounds each,
  bones and trimmings reserved
3 tablespoons grapeseed oil
1 cup mirepoix (mixed carrot, onion,
  and celery, cut into ¼-inch dice)

Pears in Wine
8 small cooking pears
2 cups full-bodied red wine
2 cups sugar
Unsalted butter

Bacon-Stuffed Cabbage (see Epigrams
  of Pigeon Breast with Bacon-Stuffed
  Cabbage, page 109)

Chestnut Confit
Oil, for deep-frying
2¼ pounds fresh chestnuts
¼ cup sugar
¼ cup brown veal stock (page 197)
¼ cup chicken stock (page 194)
Zest of 1 orange, chopped
1 celery, finely chopped
1 bay leaf

Salt and freshly ground pepper
3 stalks of fresh green peppercorns
  (from Asian grocers)
1 sprig thyme
3 bay leaves
2 tablespoons unsalted butter
¼ cup Cognac
¼ cup port
Scant ½ cup red wine
¾ cup game stock (page 196)
Scant ½ cup whipping cream

Presentation
Serve the racks of venison on a warmed serving
platter, surrounded by the stuffed cabbage, chestnut
confit, and pears, and serve the sauce separately.

Preparation

1 Brush the racks of venison with the oil, wrap them in plastic wrap, and refrigerate. Finely dice the venison bones and trimmings

2 Mix the mirepoix with the bones and trimmings.

3 To make the pears in wine, peel the pears, leaving the stems attached. Make a syrup with the wine and sugar, boil it for 5 minutes, then decrease the heat, and gently poach the pears for 20 minutes. Remove them from the syrup with a slotted spoon, transfer to a buttered baking dish, and drizzle in 1 tablespoon of the cooking syrup.

4 Prepare the bacon-stuffed cabbage as on page 109, place in a buttered baking dish, and set aside.

5 To make the chestnut confit, heat the oil in a deep-fat fryer to 350°F. Slit the chestnuts with the tip of a knife, and plunge, a few at a time into the hot oil, until the skins burst open. They are easier to peel when they are very hot, so cook in small batches. Put the sugar in a saucepan, and heat until it melts into a pale caramel. Stir in a scant ½ cup water, and the veal and chicken stocks, add the orange zest, celery, bay leaf, and the chestnuts, cover, and simmer for 30 minutes. Uncover, and cook gently for 5 to 15 minutes, until the chestnuts are meltingly tender, and the liquid is reduced and syrupy. Roll the chestnuts in this syrup from time to time, to glaze them. If necessary, add a little more water during the cooking. Leave the chestnut confit in the saucepan.

Finishing Touches and Cooking

1 Put a large roasting pan into the oven, and preheat the oven to 500°F.

2 Season the venison with salt and pepper. Pour 2 tablespoons of the oil into the roasting pan, and add the racks of venison. Roast for 5 minutes, then turn over, and add the mirepoix and trimmings mixture, the peppercorns stripped from 2 of the stalks, the thyme, and bay leaves. Roast for 3 minutes, then open the oven door, add the butter, and continue to roast for 5 minutes, basting the venison constantly with the foaming butter.

3 Remove the roasting pan from the oven, transfer the venison racks to a plate, cover with aluminum foil, and leave to rest in a warm place.

4 Decrease the oven temperature to 350°F, and cook the stuffed cabbage and the pears in wine for 7 to 8 minutes.

5 Reheat the chestnut confit.

6 Pour off the fat from the roasting pan, set it over high heat, and let the juices scorch just slightly on the bottom. Deglaze with the Cognac, port, and wine, scraping up the crust with a wooden spoon. Reduce by two-thirds, then add in the game stock, and reduce to a scant ½ cup. Add the cream, and simmer for 1 minute. Add the juices that have run out of the venison while resting, bring just to simmer, and strain through a fine sieve into a warmed sauceboat. Adjust the seasoning, and add the peppercorns stripped from the remaining stalk.

Double Veal Chops en Cocotte with Sage Tempura

Serves 4

2 veal loin chops, 1 pound each,
    well-trimmed, bones and
    trimmings reserved

Tempura Batter
$\frac{1}{2}$ egg yolk
$\frac{1}{2}$ cup ice water
Pinch of salt
1 cup superfine flour

Oil, for deep-frying
Salt and freshly ground pepper
1 tablespoon clarified butter
25 fresh sage leaves
$\frac{1}{4}$ cup unsalted butter
Scant $\frac{3}{4}$ cup brown veal stock
    (page 197)

Preparation

1   Cut the veal trimmings into very small dice.

Finishing Touches and Cooking

1   Preheat the oven to 400°F.

2   To make the tempura batter, put the egg yolk in a bowl, and beat lightly with a fork. Add the ice water, whisk lightly, then add the salt and flour, and whisk again, but do not beat the batter, which should still be grainy. Set aside.

3   Heat the deep-frying oil to 350°F.

4   Season the veal chops. Heat the clarified butter in a deep, ovenproof skillet or flame-proof baking dish, add the veal chops and their diced trimmings, and fry gently for 5 to 7 minutes on each side, until golden.

5   Add 5 sage leaves and 2 tablespoons of the butter, and place the skillet in the hot oven for 8 minutes, basting the chops at regular intervals with the foaming butter, and turning them over so that they brown evenly.

6   Remove from the oven, and transfer the chops to a plate. Cover with aluminum foil, and keep warm.

7   To make the jus, pour off the fat from the skillet, set over high heat, and deglaze the juices with $\frac{1}{4}$ cup water, scraping up the crust. Leave to evaporate, then add the veal stock, and cook for 5 minutes. Season, strain the jus, and whisk in the remaining whole butter. Serve in a sauceboat.

8   Dip 20 sage leaves into the tempura batter, then fry them in the hot oil until crisp. Drain on paper towels, and season with salt.

Presentation
Present the chops on a plate, either whole or carved,
and garnish with the fried sage leaves.

Venison Cutlets and Fillets with Juniper Cream Sauce

Preparation

1 Crush the juniper berries.

2 Brush the venison cutlets and fillets with 2 tablespoons of the oil, sprinkle with half of the crushed juniper and all the thyme leaves, place on a plate, cover with plastic wrap, and refrigerate.

3 Mix the venison trimmings with the mirepoix.

4 To make the juniper cream sauce, heat the remaining 1 tablespoon of the oil in a deep skillet, add the mirepoix mixture and the remaining crushed juniper, and cook until well browned. Deglaze with the wine, reduce, and add the game stock. Decrease the heat, and gently reduce by half. Stir in the cream, and simmer for 5 minutes. Strain through a fine sieve into a clean saucepan, season with salt, pepper, and Cognac, and set aside.

Finishing Touches

1 Reheat the cream sauce.

2 Heat the remaining oil in a large skillet.

3 Season the venison pieces with salt and pepper.

4 Place the venison in the skillet, and cook over high heat for 2 minutes on each side. Add the butter, and cook for another minute, basting the meat continuously with the foaming butter. Remove the skillet from the heat, and leave to rest in a warm place, covered with aluminum foil.

5 Deglaze the skillet with 1 to 2 tablespoons of water, and add this to the sauce. Add the gin, and bring just to a simmer. Season.

Serves 4

10 juniper berries
8 venison cutlets, $3/4$ inch thick
2 venison filets mignons
3 tablespoons grapeseed oil
Leaves from 1 sprig thyme
4 ounces venison trimmings, diced
$1/2$ cup mirepoix (mixed carrot, onion, and celery, cut into $1/4$-inch dice)
$1/4$ cup white wine
Scant $1/2$ cup game stock (page 196)
Scant $1/2$ cup whipping cream
Salt and freshly ground pepper
Dash of Cognac
4 teaspoons unsalted butter
1 tablespoon gin

Presentation
Cut the fillets into $1^1/4$-inch-thick slices, and arrange on a platter with the cutlets opposite. Pour the sauce around the venison. Accompany the dish with buttered fresh noodles, chestnut confit, Brussels sprouts, or whatever you like.

Confit Shoulder of Scottish Lamb with Lemon

Serves 4

3 lemons

1 cup fresh Italian parsley

3 tablespoons grapeseed oil

2 shoulders of Scottish lamb,
  2 pounds each, boned (with the
  end of the bone left on) and tied

Salt and freshly ground pepper

3 sprigs thyme

5 cloves garlic, unpeeled

1 cup mirepoix (mixed carrot, onion,
  and celery, cut into ¼-inch dice)

1¼ cups brown veal stock (page 197)

2 tablespoons unsalted butter

Preparation

1 Scrub one of the lemons under hot water, dry thoroughly, and peel off the zest in long strips, using a swivel peeler. With a small, very sharp knife, cut off and discard all the white pith from underneath the zest. Bring a small saucepan of water to a boil, add the strips of zest, bring back to a boil, and blanch for 2 minutes. Drain, refresh in cold water, and drain again.

2 Finish peeling the same lemon, removing all the white pith, and cut the flesh into segments between the membrane. Wrap in plastic wrap, and set aside.

3 Squeeze the juice of the other 2 lemons, and set aside.

4 Chop the blanched lemon zest and the parsley leaves, mix together, place in a small airtight container, and set aside.

Cooking

1 Place the oil in a roasting pan, place the pan in the oven, and preheat the oven to 425°F.

2 Season the lamb with salt and pepper. Place in the roasting pan with the thyme and garlic, and roast for 30 minutes, turning the meat over to brown well on all sides.

3 Add the mirepoix, and cook for 8 minutes to brown, stirring. Remove the roasting pan from the oven, and place the lamb on a plate.

4 Decrease the oven temperature to 350°F.

5 Pour off the fat from the roasting pan, set the pan over high heat, and deglaze with ¾ cup of water and the reserved lemon juice, scraping up all the crust from the bottom of the pan. Reduce by one-third. Add the veal stock, return the lamb to the roasting pan, and roast in the oven for 1¼ hours, basting frequently. If the jus becomes too thick, dilute it with a little water.

6 Transfer the cooked lamb to a warmed serving platter, and keep warm.

7 Set the roasting pan over high heat, scrape up the crust from the bottom with a wooden spoon, bring just to a simmer, adjust the seasoning, and strain through a fine sieve into a sauceboat.

8 Heat the butter in a skillet until foaming, add the lemon zest and parsley mixture, and pour it over the lamb.

Presentation
Serve the lamb shoulders whole, surrounded by the lemon segments. Serve the jus separately. Accompany the dish with a gratin of cardoons, braised Belgian endives, or any other seasonal vegetables.

Curried Shoulder of Lamb with Golden Raisins

Serves 4

Scant ³/₄ cup golden raisins
1 red bell pepper
1 yellow bell pepper
4 tablespoons medium or strong
    curry powder
1 tablespoon all-purpose flour
Salt
2 onions
1 Reinette or Cox apple
2¹/₄ pounds boned shoulder of lamb,
    cut into 1¹/₂-inch cubes
2 tablespoons grapeseed oil
1¹/₄ cups white wine
1¹/₄ cups chicken stock (page 194),
    plus more as needed
1 tablespoon olive oil
Scant ³/₄ cup whipping cream
Freshly ground pepper
Basmati Rice Pilaf (see Roast Guinea
    Fowl with Indian Spices, Deep-
    Fried Herbs, and Basmati Rice Pilaf,
    page 115), for serving

Preparation

1   Soak the golden raisins in a bowl of hot water.
2   Peel the bell peppers with a swivel peeler, open them up, remove the seeds and white ribs, then cut into ¹/₈-inch dice. Place in an airtight container, and keep cool.
3   In a large plastic bag, mix the curry powder, flour, and 2 teaspoons salt.
4   Peel and chop the onions, place in an airtight container, and keep cool.
5   Peel and core the apple, and cut into ¹/₂-inch dice. Wrap in plastic wrap, and keep cool.

Cooking

1   Preheat the oven to 400°F.
2   In batches, add the lamb pieces to the bag of curry mixture, and shake to coat.
3   Quickly heat the grapeseed oil in a large skillet, add the lamb, and brown well on all sides. Add the onion halfway through.
4   When the lamb is well browned, remove the lamb and onion with a slotted spoon, and place in a flame-proof casserole.
5   Pour off the fat from the skillet, and deglaze the pan with the wine and chicken stock. Do not reduce, but pour the liquid over the lamb, making sure it is well covered. Add a little more stock if necessary.
6   Add the apple, cover the casserole, and cook in the oven for 1¹/₂ to 2 hours. Remove the lid after 1 hour, and press the meat occasionally to check if it is cooked. If it gives to the touch, it is ready. Remove from the casserole with a slotted spoon, transfer to a serving dish, and keep warm.
7   Drain the golden raisins. Heat the olive oil in a skillet, add the bell peppers, sauté for 3 to 4 minutes, and season. Remove the skillet from the heat, and add the raisins.
8   Put the casserole over low heat, and finish the sauce by stirring in the cream. Bring to a boil, simmer for 1 minute, and reduce the sauce if there seems too much. Season with salt and pepper, and strain through a sieve over the lamb. Scatter the bell peppers and raisins over the top of the lamb.

Presentation
Serve on a large platter, or on separate plates with
basmati rice pilaf, or Creole rice.

Saddle of Hare with Paprika and Braised Red Cabbage

Preparation

1 Make a deep cut all along the length of the saddles on either side of the backbone, leaving 1¼ inches uncut at each end. Push a sprig of thyme into each incision, dust the saddles with paprika, wrap in plastic wrap, and refrigerate.

2 Mix the hare trimmings with the mirepoix, cover, and keep cool.

3 Peel and finely chop the shallot, place in a small airtight container, and keep cool.

4 To prepare the red cabbage, tie the clove, peppercorns, and bay leaf in a piece of muslin.

5 Peel, core, and quarter the apple, and slice it thinly.

6 Trim the cabbage, cut out and discard the large ribs, and slice the leaves into ¼-inch-wide strips. Peel and thinly slice the onion. Heat the clarified butter in a casserole, add the cabbage and onion, and cook for 5 minutes. Add the bag of spices and the bacon rind, pour in the chicken stock, and bring to a boil. Cover, decrease the heat to very low, and simmer for 15 minutes, stirring occasionally. Add the apple, and continue to cook for another 15 minutes, until the cabbage is well cooked, but not falling apart. Season with salt and pepper, and set aside.

Finishing Touches

1 Preheat the oven to 500°F.

2 Reheat the cabbage with the butter, stir in the vinegar to preserve the red color, and season. Remove the spice bag and bacon rind.

3 Season the saddles of hare with salt and pepper.

4 If necessary, reheat the chestnut confit.

5 Heat the oil in a roasting pan until very hot, add the trimmings and mirepoix mixture, and cook for 3 minutes. Push the mixture to the side of the pan, add ¼ cup of the butter and, as soon as it is foaming, add the saddles, resting on one fillet. Cook for 1 minute, then turn them onto the other fillet, and cook for 1 minute. Lay the saddles flat on the bones, and place the roasting pan in the oven. Roast for 8 minutes, basting 2 or 3 times with the butter.

6 Open the oven door, and set the roasting pan on or just inside the door. Dust each saddle with ½ tablespoon of paprika, and leave to rest for 6 or 7 minutes, basting frequently with the cooking juices.

7 Transfer the saddles to a platter, fillet-side down. Cover with aluminum foil, and keep warm on the open oven door.

8 Pour off the fat from the roasting pan, deglaze the pan with a scant ¾ cup water, scraping up the crust, reduce by half, and remove from the heat.

9 To make the sauce, in a small saucepan, gently cook the shallot with 2 teaspoons of the butter and 1 teaspoon of the paprika, until very soft. Add the juices from the roasting pan and the game stock, and reduce by half. Stir in the sour cream, mustard, and a good dash of the vinegar, and bring just to a simmer. Check the seasoning, and whisk in the remaining butter. Pour into a warmed sauceboat.

10 Slice the hare fillets from the bones, and slice each one thinly.

Serves 4

2 saddles of hare, trimmings cut into small pieces
4 sprigs thyme
2½ tablespoons paprika
1 cup mirepoix (mixed carrot, onion, and celery, cut into ¼-inch dice)
1 shallot

Braised Red Cabbage
1 clove
10 black peppercorns
½ bay leaf
1 apple
2¼ pounds red cabbage
1 small onion
2 tablespoons clarified butter
2 ounces smoked bacon rind
2¼ cups chicken stock (page 194)
Salt and freshly ground pepper
4 teaspoons unsalted butter
1 tablespoon red wine vinegar

Chestnut confit (see Roast Rack of Venison with Fresh Green Peppercorns, page 124)
1 tablespoon grapeseed oil
Scant ½ cup unsalted butter
1⅓ tablespoons paprika
Scant ¾ cup game stock (page 196)
Scant ½ cup sour cream
Pinch of English mustard powder
Red wine vinegar

Presentation
Arrange the sliced fillets in a fan on warmed plates. Place the braised cabbage in the center, with a few chestnuts on top. Drizzle with a little sauce, and serve the rest of the sauce separately.

131

Fillets of Lamb with a Truffle and Parsley Crust and Périgueux Sauce

Serves 4

10 ounces fresh Italian parsley
1¹/₂ ounces fresh black truffle

Périgueux Sauce
2 ounces fresh black truffle (or truffle
   peelings)
¹/₂ shallot
3 tablespoons unsalted butter
1 tablespoon port
1 tablespoon Madeira
Scant ¹/₂ cup chicken stock
   (page 197)
Scant ³/₄ cup brown veal stock
   (page 197)

1 ounce terrine of foie gras

Parsley as a Vegetable
1 pound 2 ounces fresh Italian parsley
1 small shallot
1 tablespoon unsalted butter
Salt and freshly ground pepper
¹/₄ cup heavy whipping cream

1 egg
8 lamb cutlets
2 well-trimmed lamb fillets
2 tablespoons all-purpose flour
2 tablespoons clarified butter
1 tablespoon unsalted butter

Preparation

1 Pick off the parsley leaves, and finely chop them and the truffle. Mix, place in a small airtight container, and keep cool.

2 To make the Périgueux sauce, chop the truffle, and peel and chop the shallot. Heat 2 tablespoons of the butter in a saucepan until foaming, add the truffle and shallot, and cook gently until the shallot is translucent. Deglaze with the port and Madeira, reduce until almost dry, then add the chicken and veal stocks. Reduce by one-third, and set aside.

3 Press the foie gras through a sieve to make a purée, place in an airtight container, and keep cool.

4 To make the parsley as a vegetable, discard the thickest stalks, and wash the parsley several times. Bring a large saucepan of water to a boil, add the parsley, and cook for 6 minutes from the time the water returns to a boil. Drain, refresh in cold water, and drain again. Dry the parsley thoroughly. Peel and finely chop the shallot, place in a saucepan with the butter, and cook over medium heat until translucent. Add the parsley, and stir with a fork to untangle it. Season with salt and pepper, stir in the cream, bring to a simmer for 1 minute just to bring it together, then remove from the heat, and set aside.

Finishing Touches

1 Break the egg into a shallow bowl, and beat lightly with a fork.

2 Put the truffle and parsley mixture into a second shallow bowl.

3 Season all the lamb with salt and pepper, dust them lightly with flour, and dip them first in the egg, then in the truffle and parsley mixture. Press to help the mixture adhere.

4 Heat the clarified butter in a skillet until very hot, add all the lamb, and cook for 2 to 3 minutes on each side. Add the 1 tablespoon whole butter, and cook for 1 minute longer, basting the lamb with the foaming butter.

5 At the same time, reheat the parsley as a vegetable.

6 Reheat the Périgueux sauce base, stir in the puréed foie gras, then whisk in the remaining 1 tablespoon butter to refine the sauce. Adjust the seasoning, and pour into a warmed sauceboat.

Presentation
Arrange 2 cutlets and half a fillet on each warmed plate. Shape the parsley into quenelles, and add it to the plates. Drizzle a little of the sauce on the side of the plates, and serve the rest separately. Accompany the dish with fondant, sauté, or darphin potatoes, or perhaps a rösti.

Saddle of Lamb with Kidneys, Garlic, and Rosemary

4 lambs' kidneys

Salt and freshly ground pepper

Scant ⅓ cup unsalted butter

½ cup curly parsley

2 small sprigs rosemary

6 cloves garlic, unpeeled

2 shallots

2 tablespoons olive oil

1 saddle of lamb (ask the butcher to choose a saddle with the longest possible fillets, and to bone it out, taking care not to puncture the fatty part; and to remove the exterior and interior membranes and sinews; and to flatten the flanks and pound them slightly)

1 cup mirepoix (mixed carrot, onion, and celery, cut into ¼-inch dice)

Scant ½ cup lamb stock (page 195)

Guérande *fleur de sel*, for garnish

Coarsely crushed black peppercorns, for garnish

Preparation

1 Remove the skin from around the kidneys, and season them. Heat 4 teaspoons of butter in a skillet until very hot, add the kidneys, sear for 30 seconds, and drain.

2 Finely chop the parsley leaves and the leaves from 1 branch of the rosemary. Peel and finely chop 1 clove of the garlic and the shallots. Put everything in a skillet with 1 tablespoon of the olive oil, season with salt and pepper, and cook until the shallot is translucent.

3 Lay the boned saddle of lamb on a chopping board, fat-side down. Season with salt and pepper, and spread the herb mixture all over. Place the kidneys between the fillets, roll the lamb up as tightly as possible, and tie with a string in several places. Place on a plate, cover with plastic wrap, and refrigerate.

Finishing Touches and Cooking

1 Put the remaining 1 tablespoon olive oil in a roasting pan, place the pan in the oven, and preheat the oven to 475°F.

2 Season the rolled saddle of lamb.

3 Put the lamb in the hot roasting pan, and roast for 10 minutes. Surround it with the mirepoix, and add the remaining rosemary branch, the 5 remaining cloves of the garlic, and 2 tablespoons of the butter. Continue to roast for another 20 to 25 minutes, giving the lamb a quarter-turn every 5 minutes, so that it browns evenly. Baste frequently with the cooking juices during the last 10 minutes.

4 When the lamb is cooked, transfer it to a platter, cover with aluminum foil, and leave to rest on the open oven door.

5 Pour off the fat from the roasting pan, set over high heat, and deglaze with 1¼ cups of water, scraping up the crust. Reduce by two-thirds, then add the lamb stock, and reduce again by one-third. Strain through a fine sieve into a small saucepan.

6 Press to a purée 3 of the garlic cloves that were cooked with the lamb. Add all or some of this purée to the jus, place over a low heat, and whisk in 4 teaspoons of the butter. Season, and pour into a sauceboat.

7 Cut the lamb into ¾-inch thick slices.

Presentation

Arrange the slices of lamb on warmed plates, and sprinkle with the *fleur de sel* and the crushed peppercorns. Serve the jus separately. Accompany with buttered French beans or any other seasonal vegetable.

Saddle of Venison with Shallots, Juniper, and Buttered Cabbage

Preparation

1 Crush the juniper berries.

2 Brush the venison with a little of the oil, and dust with half of the crushed juniper. Add the thyme and bay leaf, wrap in plastic wrap, and refrigerate.

3 Mix the venison trimmings and the remaining crushed juniper with the mirepoix, cover with plastic wrap, and keep cool.

4 Preheat the oven to 300°F.

5 Make a light incision along the length of the unpeeled shallots. Wrap each one separately in aluminum foil, adding a tiny piece of the butter, salt, and pepper. Cook in the oven for 1 hour, remove, and set aside still wrapped.

6 To make the buttered cabbage, discard the outer leaves of the cabbage. Separate the inner leaves, and blanch for 2 minutes in a large saucepan of boiling salted water. Drain, refresh in cold water, and drain again, first in a sieve, then on a cloth.

7 Chop the onion very finely, place in a saucepan with 2 tablespoons of the butter, and cook over medium heat until translucent. Tear the cabbage leaves into uneven pieces, and add them to the pan. Cook, uncovered, for 6 to 7 minutes, adding the chicken stock a little at a time.

Cooking

1 Put the remaining oil in a roasting pan, place the pan in the oven, and preheat it to 500°F.

2 Reheat the cabbage with 2 tablespoons of the butter, and season.

3 Season the venison with salt and pepper.

4 Lay the venison, resting on one fillet, in the very hot oil in the roasting pan. Roast for 5 minutes, then turn onto the other fillet, and roast for 5 minutes. Add the mirepoix mixture and the remaining butter, and turn the venison flat onto the bones. Continue to roast for another 10 minutes, basting frequently with the butter.

5 Turn off the oven, remove the venison, place on a plate, and leave to rest on the open oven door. Put the wrapped shallots in the oven to warm them.

6 Pour off the fat from the roasting pan, set the pan over high heat, and deglaze with the wine and almost all of the gin, scraping up the crust. Add the game stock, and simmer for 10 minutes. Strain the sauce through a sieve lined with damp muslin or double cheesecloth into a small saucepan, and reduce to a scant 1/2 cup. Whisk in 4 1/2 tablespoons of the butter, and season with salt, pepper, and a dash of the remaining gin. Pour into a warmed sauceboat.

7 Unwrap the shallots, and press gently between two fingers to slip off their skins.

8 Carve off the venison fillets, and slice into medallions.

Serves 4

10 juniper berries

2 3/4 pounds saddle of venison, trimmed of all skin and sinews, sides cut to the same length, trimmings cut into small pieces

2 tablespoons grapeseed oil

1 sprig thyme

1 bay leaf

1 cup mirepoix (mixed carrot, onion, and celery, cut into 1/4-inch dice)

12 small shallots, unpeeled

9 tablespoons unsalted butter

Salt and freshly ground pepper

Buttered Cabbage

1 savoy cabbage, 1/4-pound, cored

1 small onion

1/4 cup unsalted butter

Scant 1/2 cup chicken stock (page 194)

Scant 1/2 cup full-bodied red wine

1/4 cup gin

Scant 1/2 cup game stock (page 196)

Presentation
Place a mound of buttered cabbage in the center of 4 warmed plates, and arrange the venison medallions in a fan on top. Garnish with 3 baked shallots and a few drizzles of sauce. Serve the rest of the sauce separately.

Roast Saddle of Hare with Spices and Sauterne Cream

Serves 4

2 saddles of hare, trimmings reserved

1 stalk parsley

10 juniper berries

1 clove garlic

1 cup mirepoix (mixed carrot, onion, and celery, cut into ¼-inch dice)

4 sprigs thyme

2 Reinette or Cox apples

Chestnut Confit
  (see Roast Rack of Venison with Fresh Green Peppercorns, page 124)

Bacon-Stuffed Cabbage
  (see Epigrams of Pigeon Breast with Bacon-Stuffed Cabbage, page 109)

Salt and freshly ground pepper

12 pinches of mixed spice (page 200)

1 tablespoon grapeseed oil

6½ tablespoons unsalted butter

Pinch of salt

Pinch of sugar

Scant ¾ cup Sauterne

Scant ½ cup whipping cream

Juice of ½ lemon

Preparation

1 Cut the hare trimmings into small pieces. Cut the parsley stalk into 6 pieces, lightly crush the juniper berries, and peel the garlic. Mix everything with the mirepoix, wrap in plastic wrap, and keep cool.

2 Make a deep incision in the saddles of hare on either side of the back bone, leaving about 1¼ inches uncut at each end. Push a sprig of thyme into each incision, wrap the hare in plastic wrap, and refrigerate.

3 Peel, quarter, and core the apples, wrap in plastic wrap, and keep cool.

Finishing Touches

1 Preheat the oven to 500°F.

2 Reheat the chestnut confit and stuffed cabbage.

3 Season the saddles of hare with salt and pepper, and sprinkle each one with 6 pinches of the mixed spice.

4 Heat the oil in a roasting pan until very hot, then add 4 tablespoons of the butter and the mirepoix mixture, and brown for 3 minutes.

5 Push the mirepoix to one side of the roasting pan, and add the saddles of hare, laying them on one fillet. Cook for 1 minute, then turn onto the other fillet, and cook for 1 minute. Turn flat onto the bones, and roast in the oven for 8 minutes, basting two or three times with the butter.

6 Open the oven door, stand the roasting pan on the door, and leave the hare to rest for 6 to 7 minutes, basting it frequently with the cooking butter. Turn off the oven. Transfer the saddles to a platter, flesh-side down, cover with aluminum foil, and leave to rest on the open oven door.

7 To pan-fry the apples, heat 1½ tablespoons of the butter in a skillet until hot, add the apples, sprinkle with the salt and the sugar, and fry until golden.

8 Pour off the fat from the roasting pan, set the pan over high heat, deglaze with ¾ cup water, reduce by half, and strain through a fine sieve into a small saucepan.

9 Place the saucepan over high heat, add the Sauterne, and reduce by half. Add the cream, and reduce again by half. Season with salt, pepper, and a few drops of lemon juice, then whisk in 1 tablespoon of the butter. Add the juice that has seeped out of the hare while it was resting, and pour the sauce into a warmed sauceboat.

10 Carve off the hare fillets, and slice them thinly.

Presentation
Arrange the slices of hare in a fan on warmed plates, with 2 apple quarters, stuffed cabbage, and a little of the chestnut confit. Garnish with a few drizzles of sauce, and serve the rest of the sauce separately.

T-bone Steaks with Shallots and Black Pepper

Serves 4

5 shallots

Red Wine Sauce (optional)
1 shallot
2 teaspoons unsalted butter
1 clove garlic, peeled and crushed
1 sprig thyme
Scant $^3/_4$ cup brown veal stock
(page 197)
$1^1/_2$ cups full-bodied red wine

2 T-bone steaks, $1^3/_4$ pounds each,
trimmings reserved and chopped
Salt and freshly ground pepper
2 tablespoons grapeseed oil
9 tablespoons unsalted butter
2 tablespoons coarsely ground black
peppercorns

Preparation

1 Peel and finely chop the shallots, place in an airtight container, and keep cool.

2 To make the red wine sauce, peel and finely chop the shallot, and place in a saucepan with 2 teaspoons of the butter, the crushed garlic, and the thyme. Set over medium heat, cook until the shallot is translucent, then pour in the veal stock and wine, and reduce by three-fourths, to a scant $^3/_4$ cup of liquid. Strain through a sieve into a clean saucepan, and set aside.

Finishing Touches and Cooking

1 Preheat the oven to 425°F.

2 Season the steaks with salt and pepper.

3 Heat the oil in a large roasting pan until very hot. Add the steaks and sear quickly for 3 minutes, then turn them over, and sear for 3 minutes on the other side.

4 Add 2 tablespoons of the butter, and cook the steaks in the oven for 6 minutes, basting frequently. Turn them over, and cook for another 6 minutes, still basting. Take care that the butter does not blacken; if it does, spoon it off and use fresh butter.

5 Remove the steaks from the roasting pan, place on a platter, cover with aluminum foil, and leave to rest on the open oven door.

6 Reheat the sauce, and thicken it by whisking in 3 tablespoons of the butter. Adjust the seasoning, and keep warm.

7 Pour off the fat from the roasting pan, add 4 tablespoons of the butter, the chopped shallot and coarsely ground peppercorns, and cook over medium heat until the shallots are meltingly tender. Coat the steaks with this mixture.

8 Replace the roasting pan over very high heat, and deglaze the crust and the juices with $^1/_2$ cup of water. Reduce to 1 tablespoon, and pour into the pan of sauce. Add the juices that have seeped out of the steaks while they were resting.

Presentation
Serve the steaks on a warmed platter, and the sauce in a sauceboat. Accompany with green vegetables and a potato gratin.

Variety Meats

Veal Kidney Curry

Serves 4

2 veal kidneys, 14 ounces each

About 2 tablespoons Madras curry
   powder

1 medium onion

1 small Reinette or Cox apple

1 tablespoon clarified butter

4 teaspoons all-purpose flour

Scant $^1/_2$ cup chicken stock
   (page 194)

$^3/_4$ cup whipping cream

1 bouquet garni (fresh thyme,
   parsley, and bay leaf)

Salt and freshly ground pepper

Juice of $^1/_2$ lemon

1 large onion

1 cup fresh Italian parsley

$^1/_4$ cup pine nuts

$^1/_2$ red bell pepper

Oil, for deep-frying

$3^1/_2$ tablespoons unsalted butter

$^1/_2$ tablespoon grapeseed oil

Basmati Rice Pilaf, (see Roast Guinea
   Fowl with Indian Spices, Deep-
   Fried Herbs, and Basmati Rice Pilaf,
   page 115), for serving

Preparation

1 Remove all the fat from the kidneys, and cut them into $^3/_4$-inch cubes, following the line of the lobes. Remove the tubes. Dust the kidneys with 1 teaspoon of the curry powder, place on a plate, cover with plastic wrap, and refrigerate.

2 Peel and chop the medium onion. Peel and core the apple, and cut into $^1/_8$-inch dice.

3 Heat the clarified butter in a deep skillet, add the chopped onion, and sprinkle with 1 tablespoon (level or heaping, according to taste) of the curry powder. Stir to distribute the curry, and cook until it scorches just slightly on the bottom of the skillet. Add the diced apple, and cook until everything is golden, then sprinkle with 1 teaspoon of the flour, and stir to distribute it evenly. Stir in the chicken stock and cream, add the bouquet garni, and simmer over low heat for 15 minutes.

4 Strain through a fine sieve into a clean saucepan, season with salt and pepper and a few drops of lemon juice, and set aside.

5 Peel the large onion, and cut into thin rings. Place in an airtight container, and keep cool.

6 Shorten the parsley stalks, place the sprigs in an airtight container, and keep cool.

7 Put the pine nuts in a nonstick skillet, and dry-roast over medium heat. Set aside.

8 Peel the red bell pepper with a swivel peeler, cut into $^1/_4$-inch dice, blanch for 2 to 3 minutes in boiling salted water, drain, and refresh in cold water.

Finishing Touches

1 Heat the oil in a deep-fat fryer to 350°F. Flour the onion rings, and deep-fry until crisp. Drain on paper towels.

2 Decrease the temperature to 300°F, and deep-fry the parsley until crisp. Drain on paper towels.

3 Reheat the sauce, and emulsify by whisking in 4 teaspoons of the butter with a hand blender. Season.

4 Season the kidneys with salt and pepper.

5 Heat the grapeseed oil in a nonstick skillet until very hot, add the kidneys, and cook, stirring constantly, for 30 seconds. Add the remaining butter, spread the kidneys into a single layer, and cook for no more than 1 minute. Scoop the kidneys onto a plate, and pour the cooking juices into the sauce.

Presentation

Divide the sauce between 4 warmed plates, pile the kidneys in a dome on top, and surround with onion rings, deep-fried parsley, and red pepper dice. Scatter the pine nuts over the top, and serve with rice pilaf on the side.

Sweetbread Puffs with White Truffle Risotto

Serves 4

4 pieces of veal sweetbreads, 4 to
 5 ounces each
Salt and freshly ground pepper
4 teaspoons unsalted butter
1 egg yolk
4 sheets of phyllo
3 tablespoons clarified butter

White Truffle Risotto

2½ ounces Parmigiano-Reggiano, in
 one piece
¾ ounce white truffle
1 small onion
1 tablespoon olive oil
⅔ cup arborio rice
1¾ cups hot chicken stock
 (page 194)
2 tablespoons unsalted butter
2 tablespoons whipping cream

Preparation

1 Place the sweetbreads in a bowl and let stand under a trickle of cold running water for 3 to 4 hours to clean them. Using a small pointed knife, carefully peel off the membrane, and cut out the nerves, fat, and cartilage.

2 Halve the sweetbreads lengthwise, without separating the two parts, and open them up like a book. Season with salt and pepper, then roll up each sweetbread very tightly in plastic wrap to make 4 long cylinders.

3 Steam for 10 minutes.

4 Cut off one end of the plastic-wrappped package to release the juices, then roll each cylinder very tightly in aluminum foil, and refrigerate, so they will hold their shape.

5 When the sweetbreads are very cold, unwrap them, and brown very lightly in the butter, being careful to maintain their shape.

6 Put the egg yolk in a cup with 1 tablespoon water, and beat lightly to make an eggwash.

7 Spread the phyllo on the work surface, lay a sweetbread cylinder on each one, and roll up. Brush a ¾-inch line of the eggwash over and under the seam to seal it. Cut the excess dough off at the ends of the sweetbreads. Place on a plate, cover with plastic wrap, and refrigerate.

Finishing Touches and Cooking

1 Preheat the oven to 425°F.

2 To make the risotto, shave 12 thin curls of Parmigiano-Reggiano, and grate the rest.

3 Peel the truffle.

4 Peel and finely chop the onion, place in a saucepan with the olive oil, and cook over medium heat until translucent. Add the rice, and stir until translucent. Pour in enough chicken stock to cover the rice, and add the truffle peelings for flavor. Cook until the rice is tender, adding more stock from time to time as necessary.

5 When the risotto is ready, stir in the butter, the grated cheese, and the cream, to make a velvety texture. Adjust the seasoning.

6 Heat the clarified butter in a skillet until very hot, add the sweetbread puffs, and brown quickly, then transfer to the hot oven for 10 minutes.

7 Drain the sweetbread puffs on paper towels, and cut each cylinder into 3 equal pieces.

Presentation
Divide the risotto between 4 warmed plates, and shave the truffle over the tops with a truffle shaver. Stand the sweetbread puffs vertically around the risotto, and garnish with the curls of Parmigiano-Reggiano.

Roasted Veal Kidneys with Red Wine Sauce

Preparation

1 To make the sauce, peel and finely chop the shallots, and peel and crush the garlic. Place in a saucepan with 4 teaspoons of the butter, and cook over medium heat until translucent. Add the thyme and red wine, and reduce to scant $^1/_2$ cup. Add the veal stock, and bring to a boil, skimming the surface. Decrease the heat, and reduce by half.

2 Strain the reduction through a fine sieve into a small saucepan, season, and set aside.

3 To prepare the kidneys, peel and finely chop the 2 shallots.

4 Trim the kidneys, leaving on $^1/_2$ inch of fat all around. Reserve the rest of the fat. Halve the kidneys crosswise, and cut out most of the central cores. Season the cut sides, brush lightly with the butter, scatter with a few thyme leaves and the chopped shallots.

5 Spread the reserved fat from the kidneys across the bottom of an ovenproof casserole. Lay the kidneys cut-side up on the bed of fat. Cover with plastic wrap, and refrigerate.

Finishing Touches

1 Preheat the oven to 500°F.

2 Remove the plastic wrap from the kidneys. Place the casserole in the bottom of the oven, and cook for 8 to 10 minutes. Cover the pan with a sheet of aluminum foil, leave the oven door ajar, and keep an eye on them; when the kidneys are covered with beads of blood, they are ready. Remove the casserole from the oven.

3 Raise the oven shelf to broiler height, and preheat the broiler.

4 Using a pastry brush, brush the kidneys all over with the mustard, then sprinkle the tops with the bread crumbs.

5 Reheat the sauce, and whisk in 2 tablespoons of the softened butter to thicken.

6 Just before serving, place the kidneys under the broiler for 2 minutes until golden.

Serves 4

Red Wine Sauce
2 shallots
1 clove garlic
3$^1/_3$ tablespoons unsalted butter, softened
1 sprig thyme
2 cups red Humagne wine*
Scant $^3/_4$ cup brown veal stock (page 197)

2 shallots
2 veal kidneys, about 1 pound each
Salt and freshly ground pepper
1 tablespoon unsalted butter
2 sprigs thyme
1 tablespoon strong mustard
1 to 2 tablespoons fresh white bread crumbs

*Humagne is made from a grape variety native to the Swiss canton of Valais. If it is not available, substitute a well-structured Pinot Noir, or a red wine from Languedoc or Corbières.

Presentation
Serve a half a kidney per person, preferably on a bed of leaf spinach briefly cooked in butter. Serve the sauce separately.

Crisp Sweetbreads with Port and Ginger

Serves 4

4 pieces of veal sweetbreads,
  4 to 5 ounces each
3 ounces ginger
3 tablespoons clarified butter
30 fresh tarragon leaves
1 red bell pepper
1 yellow bell pepper
Salt and freshly ground pepper
1 tablespoon whipping cream
1 tablespoon all-purpose flour
Scant ½ cup unsalted butter
¼ cup port
1 cup brown veal stock (page 197)

Preparation

1 Place the sweetbreads in a large bowl and let stand under a slow trickle of cold running water for 3 to 4 hours to clean them. Using a small pointed knife, carefully peel off the membrane, and cut out the nerves, fat, and cartilage. Place on a plate, cover with plastic wrap, and refrigerate.

2 Peel the ginger. Cut ⅓ of the ginger into long, very thin julienne, and the rest into tiny dice. Place in separate airtight containers, and keep cool.

3 Heat all the clarified butter in a skillet until very hot. Add the ginger julienne, and fry until golden and crisp. Immediately remove with a slotted spoon, and drain on paper towels.

4 Using the same butter, fry the tarragon leaves until crisp, and set them aside with the ginger on paper towels.

5 Strain the clarified butter, and reserve it for cooking the sweetbreads.

6 Peel the bell peppers with a swivel peeler, remove the seeds and white ribs, and cut into rectangles about ½ inch long and ¼ inch wide. Place in an airtight container, and keep cool.

Finishing Touches

1 Season the sweetbreads with salt and pepper, brush them with cream, and roll them in the flour.

2 Heat 2 teaspoons of the butter in a skillet, sauté the bell peppers, and season. Drain on paper towels.

3 Heat the reserved clarified butter in a nonstick skillet until very hot. Add the sweetbreads, and fry until golden brown and crisp on both sides. Pour off the fat from the skillet, decrease the heat, add 3 tablespoons of the fresh, whole butter, and cook the sweetbreads for 5 to 8 minutes longer, basting them with the foaming butter. Place on a plate, and keep warm.

4 To make the sauce, pour off the fat from the skillet, set the pan over high heat, deglaze with the port, and reduce it completely. Add the veal stock and diced ginger, and reduce to a syrupy consistency. Adjust the seasoning, whisk in the remaining butter, and strain the sauce through a fine sieve into a warm sauceboat.

Presentation
Arrange the bell peppers in the center of the plates.
Place a sweetbread on top, and pour a ribbon of sauce
around the edge. Garnish with the fried ginger julienne
and tarragon leaves.

Panaché of Veal Sweetbreads with Duck Foie Gras and Asparagus

Serves 4

2 veal sweetbreads, 4 ounces each

10 ounces raw duck foie gras

28 thin asparagus spears

7 ounces very small chanterelle
   mushrooms

1 shallot

1 tablespoon sherry vinegar

1/4 cup brown veal stock
   (page 197)

Salt and freshly ground pepper

10 fresh tarragon leaves

1 tablespoon whipping cream

1 tablespoon all-purpose flour

2 tablespoons clarified butter

Scant 1/2 cup unsalted butter

1/4 cup chicken stock
   (page 197)

Preparation

1 Place the sweetbreads in a large bowl and let stand under a slow trickle of cold running water for 3 to 4 hours to clean them. Using a small pointed knife, carefully peel off the membrane, and cut out the nerves, fat, and cartilage. Halve them lengthwise, place the slices on a plate, cover with plastic wrap, and refrigerate.

2 Cut the foie gras into 4 thick slices, remove the nerves with the tip of a small knife, place on a plate, cover with plastic wrap, and refrigerate.

3 Snap off and discard the hard ends of the asparagus stalks, cut the tips down to 2 inches, and cut the stalks on the diagonal into 1/4-inch slices.

4 Cook the asparagus tips in boiling salted water for 3 to 4 minutes, refresh in cold water, and drain.

5 Quickly wash the chanterelles, if necessary, drain, and place in a container lined with a folded cloth. Keep cool.

6 To make the sauce, peel and finely chop the shallot, place in a small saucepan with the vinegar, and reduce completely. Add the veal stock, bring to a boil, season, and set aside.

7 Snip the tarragon leaves, place in an airtight container, and keep cool.

Finishing Touches

1 Season the sweetbreads, brush them with the cream, and roll them in the flour.

2 Heat the clarified butter in a nonstick skillet until very hot. Add the sweetbreads, and fry until golden brown and crisp on both sides. Pour off the fat from the skillet, decrease the heat, add 3 tablespoons of the fresh, whole butter, and cook the sweetbreads for 5 to 7 minutes longer, basting them with the foaming butter. Transfer to a plate, and keep warm.

3 Heat a nonstick skillet until very hot, add the chanterelles, season with salt, and cook until their water has evaporated. Add 1 tablespoon of the butter, season with pepper, stir for 2 minutes, then remove from the heat.

4 Put the sliced asparagus stalks and the chicken stock in a saucepan, and cook over high heat until the stock has evaporated, then add 1 tablespoon of the butter, season, stir for 1 minute, and add the chanterelles. Sprinkle with the tarragon, and remove from the heat.

5 Reheat the asparagus tips with 2 teaspoons of the butter, and season.

6 Season and flour the foie gras slices. Heat a nonstick skillet until searingly hot, add the foie gras, and fry for 30 seconds on each side. Drain on paper towels.

Presentation
Mound the chanterelles and asparagus mixture in the center of warmed plates, and place half a sweetbread on top. Arrange the asparagus tips to one side, and top with a slice of foie gras. Drizzle the sauce on the side.

148

Lettuce-Wrapped Veal Sweetbreads with Four Peppers and Shallots

Serves 4

4 veal sweetbreads, 4 ounces each

Salt and freshly ground pepper

1 teaspoon whole white peppercorns

1 tablespoon whole green peppercorns

2 teaspoons whole pink peppercorns

1 teaspoon black peppercorns, preferably crushed

5 shallots

1 head romaine lettuce

2 tablespoons clarified butter

1/2 cup unsalted butter

Scant 1/2 cup brown veal stock (page 197)

1/4 cup chicken stock (page 194)

1/4 cup Madeira

Juice of 1/2 lemon

Preparation

1   Place the sweetbreads in a large bowl and let stand under a slow trickle of cold running water for 3 to 4 hours to clean them. Using a small pointed knife, carefully peel off the membrane, and cut out the nerves, fat, and cartilage. Pat dry with paper towels, and season with salt and pepper.

2   Coarsely crush the white and green peppercorns. Chop the pink peppercorns, and discard the small black seeds; you will only use the outer shells. If necessary, coarsely crush the black peppercorns.

3   Peel and finely chop the shallots.

4   Remove 8 attractive lettuce leaves, and blanch them for 1 minute in boiling salted water. Refresh in cold water and cut out the central rib. Take 2 leaves at a time, and lay them out flat on a cloth, overlapping slightly to make 4 large rectangular wrappers.

5   Heat the clarified butter in a nonstick skillet until very hot. Add the sweetbreads, and fry until golden brown and crisp on both sides. Pour off the fat from the skillet, decrease the heat, add 3 tablespoons of the fresh, whole butter, three-fourths of the shallots and all the crushed peppercorns, and cook the sweetbreads for 5 minutes, basting with this mixture. Transfer the sweetbreads to a plate.

6   Spread the shallot and peppercorn mixture left behind in the skillet over the lettuce leaves. Place a sweetbread on top, and fold over the lettuce to enclose them tightly. Place on a plate, cover with plastic wrap, and set aside.

7   To make the sauce, put the remaining uncooked shallots in a small saucepan with 2 teaspoons of the butter, and cook over medium heat until translucent. Add the veal stock, chicken stock, and Madeira and reduce gently for 5 minutes. Season with salt, pepper, and a few drops of lemon juice. Strain through a fine sieve into a clean saucepan, and set aside.

Finishing Touches

1   Preheat the oven to 400°F.

2   Brush the lettuce-wrapped sweetbreads with butter, place on a baking sheet, and cook in the oven for 10 minutes.

3   Reheat the sauce, and whisk in the remaining butter.

Presentation
Cut each lettuce-wrapped sweetbread into 3 or 4 pieces, arrange in the center of each warmed plate, and pour a ribbon of sauce around. If you wish, serve with a potato gratin dauphinois.

Whole Roast Veal Kidneys with Bay Leaves, Juniper, and Cardoon Gratin

Serves 4

7 ounces pig's caul fat (crepinelle available at Asian markets)

1¹/₂ tablespoons juniper berries

2 veal kidneys, completely enclosed in their fat, about 1 pound each

5 fresh bay leaves

1 shallot

4 sprigs Italian parsley

Cardoon Gratin

2¹/₄ pounds cardoons

Juice of 1 lemon

2 tablespoons all-purpose flour

1 tablespoon salt, plus more to taste

2 tablespoons white wine vinegar

1 large shallot

1¹/₂ tablespoons unsalted butter

Freshly ground pepper

1 egg yolk

¹/₄ cup whipping cream

Ground nutmeg

1 tablespoon grapeseed oil

3 tablespoons unsalted butter

2 tablespoons Madeira

Scant ³/₄ cup brown veal stock (page 197)

1 tablespoon gin

Preparation

1 Cover the caul with water, place in the refrigerator, and leave to soak for about 1 hour, then drain and squeeze dry.

2 Coarsely crush the juniper berries.

3 Trim off the fat from the kidneys, leaving on a ¹/₂-inch layer all over. Reserve the trimmed fat.

4 Spread out half of the caul on a cloth. Place 1 kidney close to one edge, put 2 bay leaves and half of the crushed juniper on top, and roll up the caul to enclose the kidney, making sure that it is all well protected by the fat; if not, fill in the gaps with the reserved kidney-fat trimmings. Prepare the other kidney in the same way. Wrap the kidneys in plastic wrap, and refrigerate.

5 Peel and finely chop the shallot, place in an airtight container, and keep cool.

6 Pick off the parsley leaves, place in an airtight container, and keep cool.

7 To make the cardoon gratin, cut off the hard outer leaves and base of the cardoons, and separate the tender leaves. Tear the leaves up, cut the ribs into 2¹/₄-inch pieces, and immediately drop them all into a bowl of cold water acidulated with the lemon juice to prevent discoloration.

8 To cook the cardoons, mix the flour a little at a time into 6 cups of cold water, add 1 tablespoon salt and vinegar, and bring to a boil, stirring. Add the cardoons, and cook for about 45 minutes; the cooking time will vary according to their freshness and quality. Drain.

9 Peel and finely chop the large shallot, place in a saucepan with the butter, and cook gently until translucent. Add the cardoons, season with salt and pepper, and as soon as they are hot, remove the pan from the heat. Arrange the cardoons in a gratin dish.

10 Put the egg yolk in a large bowl, whisk it a little with a fork.

11 Pour the cream into the saucepan in which you cooked the cardoons, and reduce it by half. Season with nutmeg, salt, and pepper. Whisking the egg yolk continuously, slowly pour in the reduced cream, then pour this mixture over the cardoons. Set aside.

Finishing Touches and Cooking

1 Preheat the oven to 475°F.

2 Pour the oil into a roasting pan, and place over high heat. Season the kidneys, put them in the pan, and brown quickly all over. Baste them with the fat they have rendered, put the pan in the hot oven, and roast the kidneys for 20 minutes, basting them several times with their fat. Transfer the kidneys to a platter, cover tightly with aluminum foil, and leave to rest for 7 to 8 minutes.

3 Put the cardoon gratin in the top of the oven, and brown for 15 minutes.

4 Pour off the fat from the roasting pan, set it over medium heat, and add 1¹/₂ tablespoons of the butter, the shallot, the rest of the juniper, and the last bay leaf, torn into pieces. Scrape up the crust from the bottom of the pan. When the shallot is completely translucent, add the Madeira, let it evaporate completely, then pour in the stock, decrease the heat, and simmer for 5 minutes. Strain the contents of the pan through a sieve into a small saucepan, and add the gin and the juices that have run out of the kidneys while they were resting. Bring just to a simmer, whisk in the remaining butter, and season.

5 Cut the kidneys into 3-inch-thick slices.

Presentation
Arrange the sliced kidneys on warmed plates, pour a ribbon of sauce around, and garnish with the parsley leaves. Serve the rest of the sauce and the cardoon gratin separately.

Sauté of Veal Kidneys with Truffles and Port

Preparation

1 Remove all the fat from the kidneys, and cut the meat into ³/₄-inch cubes, following the line of the lobes. Cut out the cores, place the cubed kidneys on a plate, and cover with plastic wrap.

2 Coarsely chop the truffle, place in an airtight container, and keep cool.

3 Peel and finely chop the shallot, and place in a saucepan with 2 teaspoons of the butter. Cook until translucent, add the port, and reduce completely, then pour in the veal stock and the cream, and simmer gently until reduced to ³/₄ cup. Strain through a fine sieve into a saucepan large enough to hold the kidneys, season with salt and pepper, and set aside.

Finishing Touches

1 To make the pasta, fill a saucepan with abundant water, add plenty of salt and the oil, and bring to a boil. Add the tagliatelle, and cook until al dente. Immediately drain, return to the dry saucepan with the butter, stir, season, and keep warm.

2 Season the kidneys.

3 Reheat the sauce, and emulsify by whisking in 3 tablespoons of butter, using a hand blender. Adjust the seasoning, and keep warm.

4 Heat the oil in a very large nonstick skillet until very hot. Add the cubed kidneys in a single layer, and the truffle, and stir continuously for 30 seconds, then add the 2 tablespoons of butter, and cook for no more than 1 minute, still stirring. Immediately scoop the contents of the skillet into the sauce.

Serves 4

4 veal kidneys, 14 ounces each
1¹/₂ ounces black truffle
1 shallot
About ¹/₃ cup unsalted butter
Scant ¹/₂ cup port
Scant ³/₄ cup brown veal stock
   (page 197)
³/₄ cup whipping cream
Salt and freshly ground pepper

Fresh Pasta Garnish
1 tablespoon grapeseed oil
14 ounces fresh tagliatelle
4 teaspoons unsalted butter

1 tablespoon grapeseed oil

Presentation
Arrange the tagliatelle in a nest on each warmed plate, and spoon the sauté of kidneys and truffle into the center.

153

Cold Desserts

Chocolate Feuillantine with Poached Pears and Kumquats

Serves 4

9¹/₂ ounces bittersweet chocolate
  (70 percent cocoa solids)

1³/₄ cups sugar

1 vanilla pod

1 tablespoon fresh lemon juice

4 slightly under-ripe pears

³/₄ cup kumquats

³/₄ cup fresh orange juice

¹/₂ cup shelled and skinned hazelnuts

4 scoops of caramel ice cream
  (page 160), for serving

Melted bittersweet chocolate,
  for decoration

Melted caramel ice cream,
  for decoration

Preparation and Finishing Touches

1 Break the chocolate into small pieces and melt it slowly, over barely simmering water, in the top of a double boiler. Cover a baking sheet with parchment paper and spread the melted chocolate evenly over it, in a thin (¹/₁₆-inch) layer. Using a 2³/₄-inch-square or triangular pastry cutter, mark out 12 shapes. Leave to rest in the refrigerator.

2 Combine 2 cups water and 1¹/₄ cups of the sugar in a saucepan. Split the vanilla pod, scrape the seeds into the saucepan, and add the split pod and the lemon juice.

3 Peel the pears and immediately plunge them into this liquid to prevent discoloration. Bring to a boil, then poach gently for 10 to 15 minutes, depending on the ripeness of the pears. Insert a knife blade into the center to check; it should slide in easily. Remove the saucepan from the heat and leave the pears to cool in the poaching syrup.

4 Quarter the kumquats and remove the seeds.

5 Combine the orange juice and the remaining ¹/₂ cup sugar in a saucepan and bring to a boil. Add the kumquat quarters, stir to mix, and poach over medium heat for 6 minutes. The fruit should still be slightly firm. Leave to cool in the syrup.

6 Preheat the oven to 350°F. On a baking sheet, toast the hazelnuts until lightly browned, watching carefully that they do not burn. Chop them coarsely and reserve.

Presentation
Place a chocolate square on each plate. Halve, core, and slice the pears. Fan out the halves and put one half on each chocolate square. Repeat with another square and another pear fan, and finally cover with a third chocolate square. Place a scoop of caramel ice cream on one side of each plate and surround it with a crown of kumquat quarters. Decorate the plates with a lattice of melted chocolate and melted caramel ice cream, and scatter the chopped hazelnuts over the top.

Watermelon Gelée

Serves 4

5 sheets leaf gelatin
3 pounds watermelon
About ²/₃ cup sugar
Juice of 1 lemon
1 grapefruit
4 sprigs mint

Preparation

1 Soften the gelatin sheets in enough cold water to cover.

2 Peel the watermelon, and reserve a little of red flesh for the garnish.

3 Cut the flesh into large cubes, remove and discard the seeds, purée the flesh in a blender, and press the purée through a fine sieve.

4 Measure out 5 cups of this watermelon juice, pour it into a saucepan, and add ¹/₂ to ²/₃ cup sugar, according to your taste and the sweetness of the watermelon. Add all but 1 teaspoon of the lemon juice, and set the saucepan over low heat until all the particles of watermelon rise to the surface.

5 Strain the juice several times through a fine sieve to make a clear liquid.

6 Measure out 7 tablespoons of the juice and pour it into a small saucepan. Squeeze the soaked gelatin with your hands to extract all the water, add it to the juice and heat, stirring, but do not let the liquid boil. As soon as the gelatin has dissolved, add the remaining watermelon juice, stir, and leave in a cool place until the jelly is half-set.

7 Peel the grapefruit, removing all the pith and membrane. Cut out 6 segments, and cut these into ¹/₈-inch dice. Place in an airtight container, and keep cool.

8 Cut the reserved watermelon into small dice, place in a bowl, and add a little sugar and a few drops of lemon juice.

9 Pour 1 tablespoon of the half-set gelée into the bottom of 4 dry martini glasses, scatter in a little diced watermelon, then add another layer of gelée, and repeat until the glasses are full. Leave to set in the refrigerator for several hours.

Presentation
Decorate each glass with some diced grapefruit and
a sprig of mint.

Wild Strawberry and Champagne Mousseline

Preparation

1 Reserve 4 ounces of the strawberries.
2 To make the mousseline, purée 10 ounces of strawberries in a blender with almost all the sugar and the lemon juice. Add the champagne, and extra sugar to taste.
3 Dip the edges of 4 glasses very lightly in lemon juice, then dip them in sugar.
4 Flake the pistachios.

Serves 4

14 ounces wild strawberries, stems removed
$^1/_4$ cup sugar, plus more for frosting
Juice of $^1/_2$ lemon, plus enough for frosting
$^2/_3$ cup champagne
$1^1/_2$ tablespoons pistachios, shelled and skinned

Presentation
Put 1 tablespoon of the reserved wild strawberries at the bottom of the glasses, and sprinkle with a little sugar if you wish. Cover with the strawberry mousseline, and garnish each glass with a strawberry and some flaked pistachios. Serve very cold.

Ice Cream

It is not possible to give precise timings for churning home-made ice cream, since they vary so much depending on the model of your ice cream maker. Ideally, they should be kept frozen between 10°F and 15°F. If your deep-freeze cannot be held at these temperatures, transfer the ice cream to the refrigerator and leave it to soften for some time before serving; again, you will need to experiment, as it could take anywhere from 30 minutes to more than an hour!

Caramel Ice Cream

³/₄ cup milk, ¹/₂ cup whipping cream, ¹/₂ vanilla bean, 5 ounces sugar cubes, 8 egg yolks

Preparation

1 Pour the milk and cream into a saucepan, add the vanilla bean, scraping out the seeds, and bring to a boil.
2 Put a little of the sugar in another saucepan, and cook without added liquid, adding more in small quantities, until you have a golden brown caramel. Remove the vanilla pod, and pour the boiling milk and cream onto the caramel, whisking to dissolve it completely.
3 Put the egg yolks in a bowl, and slowly pour on the milk mixture, whisking constantly. Return the mixture to the saucepan.
4 Set over very low heat, and cook like a crème anglaise, stirring until the custard has thickened just enough to coat the back of a spoon.
5 Strain the custard through a fine sieve into a bowl, and leave until completely cold before churning in an ice-cream maker.

Caramel Praline Ice Cream

2¹/₂ ounces praline (page 202); 9 ounces sugar cubes; 2 vanilla beans, split and each one cut into 3 pieces; ³/₄ cup heavy whipping cream; 1²/₃ cups milk; 8 egg yolks

Preparation

1 Chop the praline.
2 Put the sugar cubes and vanilla bean pieces in an enamelled saucepan set over low heat, and cook without stirring until the sugar has dissolved.
3 When the dissolved sugar begins to turn golden brown, stir with a wooden spoon over very low heat, until it becomes a dark caramel brown.
4 Remove the pan from the heat, and add the cream, stirring vigorously; be careful, as it may spatter.
5 Return the pan to very low heat, and stir with the wooden spoon until the caramel has completely dissolved. Remove from the heat.
6 Bring the milk to a boil.
7 Beat the egg yolks in a bowl, and slowly pour on the boiling milk, whisking vigorously.
8 Pour this mixture into the saucepan containing the caramel, whisking constantly. Return the pan to the heat and cook, whisking all the time, until the mixture just begins to simmer.
9 To remove the vanilla bean pieces, strain the mixture through a fine sieve, and leave until completely cold.
10 Add the chopped praline, mix, and churn in an ice-cream maker.

Almond Milk Ice Cream

1 cup italian meringue (page 200), ¹/₄ cup milk, ¹/₄ cup orgeat syrup (from Asian grocers), 1 cup whipping cream

Preparation

1 Make the italian meringue.
2 Mix the milk and orgeat syrup in a blender, and pour into an ice-cream maker.
3 Churn until the ice cream is half-frozen, then stir in the italian meringue, and churn until completely frozen.

Coconut Ice Cream

Infusion: 1$\frac{1}{2}$ tablespoons milk, 5 teaspoons superfine sugar, 1$\frac{1}{2}$ tablespoons powdered coconut milk

Ice Cream: 6 egg yolks, 1 cup superfine sugar, $\frac{1}{4}$ cup milk, $\frac{2}{3}$ cup whipping cream

Preparation

1 To make the infusion, bring the milk and sugar to a boil. Pour the boiling mixture onto the powdered coconut milk, cover the bowl with plastic wrap (for a better flavor), and leave to infuse for 2 to 3 hours.
2 To make the ice cream, put the egg yolks and sugar in a bowl, and whisk vigorously until pale.
3 Pour the milk and the coconut infusion into a saucepan, bring to a boil, and pour the boiling mixture onto the egg mixture, whisking constantly.
4 Return the mixture to the pan, place over very low heat, and cook like a crème anglaise until thickened, stirring continuously, and taking care not to let it boil.
5 When the custard is just thick enough to coat the back of a spoon, stop the cooking by adding the cream, stir to mix, and remove from the heat.
6 Let stand until completely cold, then churn in an ice-cream maker.

Hazelnut Ice Cream

$\frac{3}{4}$ cup hazelnuts, skinned; 5 egg yolks; $\frac{1}{2}$ cup sugar; $\frac{1}{4}$ cup milk; $\frac{2}{3}$ cup whipping cream; 5 ounces *praliné* mass (from confectioners)

Preparation

1 Preheat the oven to 350°F. Roast the hazelnuts in the oven, taking care that they do not brown too quickly or they will taste bitter. Chop the nuts, and reserve them to sprinkle over the ice cream just before serving.
2 To make the ice cream, combine the egg yolks and sugar in a bowl, and whisk vigorously until pale.
3 Pour the milk, cream, and *praliné* mass into a saucepan, bring to a boil, and pour over the egg yolks, whisking constantly.
4 Return the mixture to the saucepan, heat until it just begins to simmer, then strain through a fine sieve, and let stand until completely cold.
5 Pour into an ice-cream maker, and churn until frozen.

Rum and Golden Raisin Ice Cream

Scant $\frac{1}{2}$ cup golden raisins, 2 tablespoons dark rum, 3 egg yolks, $\frac{1}{2}$ cup sugar, 1 cup milk, 1 cup whipping cream

Preparation

1 Soak the golden raisins in the rum for 1 hour.
2 Put the egg yolks and sugar in a bowl, and whisk vigorously until pale.
3 Pour the milk and cream into a saucepan, bring to a boil, then pour onto the egg mixture, whisking constantly.
4 Return the mixture to the pan, place over very low heat, and cook like a crème anglaise, stirring with a wooden spoon until the custard is just thick enough to coat the back of the spoon.
5 Drain the raisins, reserving the rum. Add the rum to the custard, and strain through a fine sieve. Leave until completely cold.
6 Churn in an ice-cream maker. As soon as the mixture starts to freeze, stir in the raisins.

Strawberry and Banana Salad with Candied Citrus Zests

Serves 4

1 orange
1 lemon
1 lime
1/2 cup plus 2 to 3 tablespoons sugar
2 bananas, plus 1 not-too-ripe banana
    for garnish
8 ounces strawberries

Preparation

1   Preheat the oven to 175°F.

2   Scrub the citrus fruit under hot water, and dry thoroughly.

3   Using a swivel peeler, peel off bands of zest, and use a small pointed knife to cut off all the bitter white pith from underneath the zests. Cut the zests into the finest possible julienne.

4   Blanch the citrus julienne in boiling water for 30 seconds, and drain.

5   Pour a scant 1/2 cup water into a small saucepan, add 1/2 cup of the sugar, and bring to a boil. Add the citrus julienne, bring back to a boil, then simmer for 3 minutes, and remove from the heat. Set aside.

6   Using a mandoline or electric slicer, cut 4 long, thin slices, 1/2 inch wide, from the banana reserved for the garnish. Line a baking sheet with parchment paper, arrange the banana slices on top, and dry in the oven for 30 minutes.

7   Squeeze the juice of 1/2 lemon and 1/4 orange.

8   Wash and hull the strawberries, and drain. Choose the 12 best berries, quarter them, place in an airtight container, and keep cool.

9   Cut the 2 remaining bananas and the strawberries into 1/4-inch dice. Combine them in a large bowl, and sprinkle with the lemon and orange juice. Dust with 2 to 3 tablespoons sugar, add 2 tablespoons of the drained citrus zests, mix, and keep cool.

Presentation
Arrange the quartered strawberries around the edge of
4 plates, and place the strawberry and banana salad
in the middle. Garnish with a slice of dried banana,
and scatter with the candied citrus zests.

Pineapple Dartois

Serves 4

Scant ½ cup raisins
¼ cup rum
1 pineapple
2 tablespoons unsalted butter
½ cup granulated sugar
1 pound 2 ounces puff pastry
   (page 201)
½ cup almond paste
2 egg yolks, lightly beaten
Confectioners' sugar, for sprinkling
Rum and Golden Raisin Ice Cream
   (page 161), for serving

Preparation

1 Soak the raisins in hot water for 30 minutes, drain, and then soak them in the rum.

2 Carefully peel the pineapple, quarter it vertically, and cut out the hard central core. Cut each quarter into ½-inch-thick slices.

3 Heat a nonstick skillet, add the butter, and when it is foaming, add the pineapple slices. Add the granulated sugar, and cook over medium heat until all the liquid from the pineapple has evaporated.

4 Drain the raisins, add them to the skillet, increase the heat slightly, and lightly caramelize all the fruit. Set aside.

5 Roll out the puff pastry to a thickness of about ⅛-inch, and cut it into two 12 by 5-inch rectangles. Place on a baking sheet, and refrigerate for 20 minutes.

6 Spread the almond paste over one of the pastry rectangles, leaving a ¾-inch border all around.

7 Arrange the pineapple slices on the almond paste, and scatter the raisins on top.

8 Brush the pastry borders with the egg yolks, and place the other pastry rectangle on top. Press to seal firmly, then crimp the pastry by pressing all around the edge with the tip of a small spoon, and neaten the edge with a pastry wheel.

9 Glaze the dartois with the egg yolks, and decorate the top by tracing diamonds with the tip of a knife, taking care not to cut all the way through the pastry. Refrigerate the dartois while you preheat the oven.

Finishing Touches and Cooking

1 Preheat the oven to 475°F.

2 Bake the dartois for 15 minutes.

3 Decrease the oven temperature to 425°F, and continue to bake for another 15 to 20 minutes. Five minutes before the end of the cooking time, sprinkle the surface of the dartois with the confectioners' sugar, and continue to bake until it has a beautiful pale golden glaze.

Presentation
Serve the dartois slightly warm, or cold, with the rum and raisin ice cream.

Mousseline of White Peaches with Wild Strawberries

Preparation and Finishing Touches

Serves 4

1 Weigh out 2¼ pounds of the peaches, wash, halve, and pit them without peeling, place in a blender or food processor with half the liqueur, ⅔ cup of the sugar, and half the lemon juice, and purée.

2 Press through a fine sieve, and refrigerate.

3 Plunge the remaining peaches into a saucepan of boiling water for 15 seconds, then immediately drop them into cold water. Peel and pit them.

4 Finely dice the peaches, place in a bowl, add a little sugar, a few drops of lemon juice, and the remaining liqueur. Refrigerate.

5 Halve the pistachios lengthwise, then cut them into thin sticks.

2 pounds 14 ounces white peaches
Scant ½ cup maraschino liqueur
¾ cup sugar
Juice of 1 lemon
1½ tablespoons pistachios, skinned
8 ounces wild strawberries, hulled

Presentation
Spoon the mousseline into saucer-style champagne glasses or small Asian bowls, and garnish with the diced peaches, wild strawberries, and pistachios.

Strawberry Succès

Serves 4

Strawberry Coulis
8 ounces strawberries
7 to 9 tablespoons sugar
Juice of 1 lemon

1$^1/_2$ tablespoons pistachios, skinned
4 squares of bittersweet chocolate
   (70 percent cocoa solids)
8 small *succès* bases (from
   confectioners)
4 ounces wild strawberries
4 large scoops of Caramel Praline
   Ice Cream (page 160)
4 ounces praline (page 202)
Confectioners' sugar, for dusting

Preparation

1 To make the strawberry coulis, wash, hull, and drain the strawberries, put them in a blender or food processor with the sugar and lemon juice, and purée for 2 minutes. Press through a fine sieve to eliminate the small seeds, and refrigerate.

2 Chop the pistachios for the garnish.

Finishing Touches

1 Melt the chocolate in a double boiler over very low heat. Spread the melted chocolate over 4 of the *succès* bases, and, before it sets, cover the surface with the wild strawberries, pointing upward. The chocolate will hold them in place.

2 Lay the other 4 *succès* bases on the work surface, and place a scoop of ice cream on each one. Push a palette knife over the surface of the ice cream to flatten it slightly.

3 Very carefully press some of the praline onto the ice cream–covered bases using a spatula.

Presentation
Spread the strawberry coulis over 4 dessert plates, and place an ice cream–covered *succès* base in the middle. Cover with a strawberry-topped *succès* base. Decorate with chopped pistachios and dust with confectioners' sugar.

Nion Tart

Serves 4 to 6

10 ounces sweet shortcrust pastry
   (page 201)
1 tablespoon walnut oil
2 ounces walnut or hazelnut *nion*
Scant ½ cup milk
Scant ½ cup whipping cream
2 eggs
1 egg yolk
Scant ½ cup sugar
1 tablespoon plum jam

Preparation

1 Preheat the oven to 450°F.

2 Roll out the pastry to a thickness of about ⅛ inch. Place an 8-inch flan ring on a baking sheet brushed with the walnut oil, and line it with the pastry. Place a circle of aluminum foil inside, and fill with baking beans or dried peas. Bake blind in the oven for 25 minutes, remove, and leave to cool in the flan ring.

3 Decrease the oven temperature to 300°F.

4 Finely grate the *nion,* mix it with the milk, and let stand for 15 minutes.

5 Whisk in the cream, eggs, egg yolk, and sugar, then strain the mixture through a sieve into another bowl.

6 Add the jam, and mix with a hand blender.

7 Remove the foil and baking beans from the pastry case. Place the baking sheet and pastry case in the flan ring on the bottom shelf of the oven, and fill the pastry with the *nion* mixture.

8 Bake for 30 to 35 minutes. Push the tart gently with your finger; if the filling wobbles, cook for a few more minutes.

9 Slide the tart off the baking sheet onto a wire rack, and leave to cool before removing the flan ring.

Hot Desserts

Pineappled Dacquois with Coconut Ice Cream and Passion Fruit Coulis

Serves 4

7 ounces viennese pastry (page 202)
1 very ripe pineapple
4 tablespoons unsalted butter
Sugar
2 tablespoons pistachios, skinned

Meringue
1/4 cup egg whites
1/2 cup sugar

Passion Fruit Coulis
Scant 1/2 cup bottled passion fruit
  juice, or the juice of 1 pound
  2 ounces fresh passion fruit,
  pressed and strained
1/4 cup water
1/4 cup superfine sugar

8 quenelles of coconut ice cream
  (page 160), for serving
1 1/2 tablespoons praline (page 202),
  for decorating

Preparation

1 Preheat the oven to 400°F.

2 To make the biscuit bases, roll the pastry cut to a thickness of 5/8 inch. Using a 3/4-inch pastry cutter, cut out 4 circles, place on a baking sheet lined with parchment paper, and bake in the hot oven for 8 minutes. Set aside.

3 Peel the pineapple and quarter it lengthwise. Cut out the fibrous core, and cut the flesh into 1/2-inch dice.

4 Heat the butter in a large nonstick skillet, add the pineapple, and cook, stirring constantly, until the juices have completely evaporated. Add a little sugar, cook until the pineapple is slightly caramelized, then transfer to a plate. Leave in a cool place until cold.

5 Cut the pistachios into sticks, and set aside.

Finishing Touches

1 To make the meringue, beat the egg whites with the sugar into very firm peaks.

2 Preheat the oven to 475°F.

3 To make the coulis, mix the passion fruit juice with the 1/4 cup water and superfine sugar, and heat gently until the sugar has just dissolved. Do not let boil. Let cool.

4 To assemble the dacquois, arrange a mound of pineapple on each biscuit base.

5 Using a piping bag, cover the pineapple completely with points of meringue, piping them closely to resemble a hedgehog.

6 Place the dacquois on a baking sheet, and bake in the hot oven for 7 minutes.

Presentation
Spoon a circle of passion fruit coulis in the center of 4 plates. Place a dacquois on top, and 2 quenelles of coconut ice cream below. Decorate with the pistachios sticks and flakes of praline.

Peaches with Strawberries, Fig, and Red Wine Jam, and Citrus Sabayon

Serves 4

4 small figs
Scant ¹/₂ cup red wine
¹/₄ cup sugar
Grated zest of ¹/₂ lemon
Grated zest of ¹/₂ orange
2 tablespoons flaked almonds
4 ounces small strawberries
2 nice, ripe peaches

Citrus Sabayon
1 egg yolk
¹/₄ cup fresh lemon juice
¹/₄ cup fresh orange juice
¹/₄ cup sugar

Preparation

1 To make the fig jam, peel and dice the figs. Place in a small saucepan with the wine, sugar, and citrus zests. Bring to a boil over high heat, and cook, crushing the figs with a fork, until they have a jam-like consistency. Remove from the heat and set aside.

2 Put the flaked almonds in a nonstick skillet, set over medium heat, and toast, stirring, until lightly browned. Set aside

3 Wash, hull, and drain the strawberries. Place in an airtight container, and keep cool.

Finishing Touches

1 Peel and halve the peaches, remove the pits, and cut each half into 4 quarters. Arrange them in a circle in 4 small bowls.

2 To make the citrus sabayon, fill a large saucepan half full with water, bring to a simmer, and set a large round-bottomed metal bowl on top, submerged at least halfway into the water.

3 Add the egg yolk, citrus juices, and sugar, and whisk with an electric hand mixer or a balloon whisk until the mixture has at least quadrupled in volume.

4 Halve or quarter the strawberries.

Presentation
Spoon some fig jam into the center of each peach quarter in the bowls. Arrange the strawberries in a circle on the jam. Spoon 2 tablespoons of the citrus sabayon over the strawberries, and scatter the almonds over the top.

Pineapple and Fig Charlottes with Almond Milk Ice Cream

Preparation

1 Preheat the oven to 230°F.

2 To make the charlottes, butter 4 charlotte molds, 2³/₈ inches deep.

3 Peel the pineapple, discard the end slice, then cut four ¹/₈-inch-thick slices. Place the sugar with a scant ¹/₂ cup water in a saucepan, bring to a boil, add the pineapple slices, and cook in the syrup for 1 minute. Drain, and arrange on a baking sheet lined with parchment paper. Place in the oven, and let dry for 1 hour, then set aside.

4 Quarter the rest of the pineapple lengthwise, and remove the fibrous core. Using an electric carving knife, cut 2 of the quarters lengthwise into paper-thin slices.

5 Cut the slices crosswise into ¹/₂-inch lengths.

6 Line the charlotte molds with the pineapple slices, overlapping them and extending them up above the top of the molds slightly. If you run short of slices, cut more from the remaining pineapple quarters.

7 Cut all the remaining pineapple into ¹/₄-inch dice.

8 Peel the figs, and cut into ¹/₄-inch dice.

9 Heat the 2 tablespoons butter in a nonstick skillet, add the diced pineapple, and sauté until all the juices have evaporated. Add sugar (the amount will depend on the ripeness of the fruit), the diced fig, and the liqueur, and mix together gently.

10 Fill the molds with this mixture, and fold the overhanging pineapple slices over the top. Wrap the charlottes tightly in plastic wrap, and keep cool.

11 To make the raspberry coulis, purée the raspberries in a blender or food processor, then press through a fine sieve to eliminate the seeds. Stir in sugar to taste, cover, and keep cool.

Finishing Touches

1 Preheat the oven to 300°F.

2 Unwrap the charlottes, and cook in the oven for 10 minutes.

Serves 4

2 tablespoons unsalted butter, plus extra for greasing

1 pineapple

Scant ¹/₂ cup sugar

2 purple figs

2 tablespoons maraschino liqueur

1 cup raspberries

8 quenelles of Almond Milk Ice Cream (page 160)

Presentation
Spoon a circle of raspberry coulis in the center of 4 plates. Unmold the charlottes into the center, and place 2 quenelles of ice cream below. Decorate with a slice of dried pineapple.

Caramelized Délicatesses of Apples and Candied Lemon Zest, with Rum and Golden Raisin Ice Cream

Serves 4

8 ounces puff pastry (page 201)

1 heaping tablespoon confectioners' sugar

5 lemons

2/3 cup granulated sugar

4 Reinette or Cox apples

1/4 cup unsalted butter

4 large quenelles of Rum and Golden Raisin Ice Cream (page 161), for serving

Preparation

1   To make the *délicatesses,* preheat the oven to 500°F.

2   Divide the puff pastry into 14 pieces. Cover a chopping board with parchment paper, roll out each piece to a thickness of 1/2 inch, and sprinkle with the confectioners' sugar to give a crisp finish after baking. Refrigerate for 10 minutes on the parchment, then place (still on the paper) on a baking sheet, and bake in the hot oven, watching to see that they do not burn. Leave to cool, then cut into round *délicatesses* with a 2 3/4-inch pastry cutter.

3   To make the candied lemon zests, peel off strips of the zests with a swivel peeler, and carefully cut off the bitter white pith from the underside. Cut the zests into the finest possible julienne. Bring a saucepan of water to a boil, plunge in the julienne, and bring back to a boil. Blanch for 1 minute, and drain. Repeat the operation twice more, and drain.

4   Squeeze the juice of 2 lemons. Place in a saucepan with 1/2 cup of the granulated sugar and a scant 1/2 cup water, boil for 1 minute, then drop in the lemon julienne, and simmer gently for 10 minutes. Drain on a wire rack.

5   Squeeze the juice of 1 more lemon, and set it aside.

Finishing Touches

1   Heat the butter in a skillet until foaming. Add the remaining granulated sugar, cook until it begins to caramelize, then immediately stir in the lemon juice. Bring to a simmer, add the diced apple and candied lemon zests, and sauté briskly until the apples are tender. Take care; they cook very quickly! Remove from the heat, and drain.

Presentation

Place a *délicatesse* on one side of each plate, and top with a little of the apple and lemon zest mixture. Place another *délicatesse* on top, add more apple mixture, and finish with a third *délicatesse* to make a top. Put a quenelle of ice cream on the other side of the plate. Break the remaining *délicatesses* in half, and arrange on the plates however you like, or as in the photo. If you wish, garnish with sliced pistachios and drizzles of melted chocolate and vanilla cream.

Banana Soufflés with Lemon Syrup

Serves 4

4 lemons

1 cup granulated sugar

2 tablespoons unsalted butter

12 pistachios, skinned

4 bananas

2 eggs

Confectioners' sugar, for dusting

Preparation

1   To make the lemon syrup, scrub the lemons under hot water, and dry thoroughly. Peel off strips of zest with a swivel peeler, and carefully cut off the bitter white pith from the underside. Cut the zests into fine julienne.

2   Squeeze the juice from the lemons, and strain it through a fine sieve into a saucepan. Add 3 tablespoons water and a scant ¹/₂ cup of the granulated sugar, and bring to a boil. Drop in the lemon zest julienne, and simmer for about 5 minutes, until tender.

3   Generously butter 4 individual soufflé dishes (2³/₄ inches in diameter), and refrigerate.

4   Cut the pistachios into thin sticks, and set aside.

Finishing Touches

1   Preheat the oven to 500°F.

2   Peel the bananas. Weigh out 4 ounces, and press through a sieve to make a purée.

3   Cut the remaining bananas into thin rounds.

4   Separate the eggs.

5   Put 1 egg yolk into a small bowl, add 7 tablespoons of the granulated sugar, whisk until frothy, then mix in the banana purée. (You will not need the second egg yolk for this recipe.)

6   Beat the egg whites with the remaining granulated sugar until fairly stiff, but not too firm.

7   Stir one-third of the egg whites into the banana and yolk mixture, then fold in the remaining whites gently with a spatula, lifting the mixture, and turning the bowl as you fold.

8   Fill the soufflé dishes with this mixture, and cook in the hot oven for 4 minutes.

Presentation

Arrange overlapping rounds of banana in a semicircle to one side of each plate. Drizzle a little of the lemon syrup, and sprinkle the pistachios over the bananas. Unmold the soufflés into the center of the plates, dust with confectioners' sugar, and serve the remaining syrup separately.

Poached Pears with Orange Syrup, Plum Fritters, and Hazelnut Ice Cream

Preparation

1 To make the fritter batter, separate the egg. Mix the flour, a pinch of salt, the egg yolk, milk, and water, beat well, and leave to rest in a cool place for 1 hour. Reserve the egg white.

2 To poach the pears, peel them, leaving on the stalks, and remove the cores and seeds from the underside with a melon baller (parisienne cutter) or a small knife. Prepare a syrup with 2 cups water, 1¼ cups of the sugar, and the vanilla bean, and bring to a boil. Add the pears, and poach gently for about 10 minutes, then remove from the heat, and leave to cool in the syrup.

3 To make the plum coulis, reserve 8 of the best plums for the garnish. Halve and pit the rest. Place in a saucepan, add ½ cup of the sugar, and cook over medium heat to the consistency of a compote. Purée in a blender or food processor, then press hard through a sieve to eliminate the skins. Set aside.

4 Halve and pit the reserved plums. Keep 8 of the halves intact for the fritters, and cut the rest into ¼-inch dice. Wrap the halved and diced plums separately in plastic wrap, and keep cool.

5 In a shallow bowl, mix the cinnamon and ¼ cup of the sugar. Set aside.

6 Heat a dry nonstick skillet, add the hazelnuts, and toast over medium heat, stirring. Chop them coarsely.

7 Press the marmalade through a sieve, and add a little water to give it the consistency of a syrup.

Finishing Touches

1 Preheat the oven to 350°F.

2 Heat the butter in a nonstick skillet, add the diced plums and ¼ cup of the sugar, and cook until lightly caramelized. Remove from the heat.

3 Drain the pears, and fill the cavities with the caramelized plums. Place on a baking sheet covered with parchment paper, and cook in the hot oven for 10 minutes, basting every 2 minutes with the marmalade syrup.

4 Beat the egg white with a pinch of salt until stiff. Stir one-third into the fritter batter, then gently fold in the rest with a spatula, lifting and turning the mixture.

5 Heat the clarified butter in a nonstick skillet over very high heat.

6 Coat the plum halves in the fritter batter, drop them into the hot butter, and fry until golden brown. Drain quickly on paper towels, roll the fritters in the cinnamon and sugar mixture, and keep warm.

Serves 4

Fritter Batter
1 egg
1 cup all-purpose flour
Salt
Scant ½ cup milk
⅔ cup water

4 small pears
2¼ cups sugar
½ vanilla bean
1 pound 2 ounces small plums
1 teaspoon ground cinnamon
2 ounces shelled hazelnuts
Scant ½ cup orange marmalade
1 teaspoon unsalted butter
1¼ cups clarified butter
8 quenelles of Hazelnut Ice Cream
  (page 161)

Presentation
Spoon 2 circles of plum coulis onto each plate, and top with 2 plum fritters. Place a pear in the center, with a quenelle of ice cream on one side. Sprinkle with chopped hazelnuts.

Apple and Almond Fondants with Passion Fruit Coulis

Serves 4

Filling

1 egg

1/2 cup blanched almonds, finely
  chopped

7 tablespoons unsalted butter,
  softened

1/4 cup sugar

1 tablespoon rum

3 large eating apples

Syrup

1/4 cup water

1 1/4 cups sugar

Juice of 1 lemon

2 teaspoons unsalted butter, for
  greasing

2 passion fruit, for garnish

Passion Fruit Coulis

4 or 5 passion fruit (or, substitute
  the juice of 2 oranges and 1 lime,
  mixed with 1/2 cup sugar)

1/4 cup water

Sugar

4 pinches of flaked almonds,
  for garnish

4 pinches of confectioners' sugar,
  for garnish

Slivered pistachio nuts, (optional)

Preparation

1 Thoroughly mix all the ingredients for the filling. Set aside.

2 Peel, halve, and core the apples. Cut 2 of the apples into 1/8-inch slices, and the third one into 1/4-inch dice.

3 To make the syrup, combine the water, sugar, and lemon juice in a saucepan, and bring to a boil. Add the apple slices, poach until just translucent, and remove with a slotted spoon.

4 Poach the diced apple in the same way, and drain.

5 Butter four 2 3/4-inch-diameter ramekins or molds. Line them with the apple slices, overlapping, and extending the slices up above the top of molds. Trim the upper slices to the same height. Divide the diced apples between the ramekins, then add the almond filling to the top of the molds, and fold the overhanging slices of apple over the top.

6 Scoop out the seeds from 2 passion fruit, without pressing, and reserve for the garnish.

7 To make the coulis base, halve 4 or 5 passion fruit, and press to extract 2/3 cup of juice. Set aside.

Finishing Touches and Cooking

1 Preheat the oven to 400°F.

2 Mix the coulis base with the 1/4 cup water and sugar to taste, and heat gently until the sugar has just dissolved. Do not let it boil.

3 Cook the fondants in the hot oven for 12 minutes. Remove, and raise the oven shelf to the broil position.

4 Unmold the fondants onto a sheet of buttered parchment paper, sprinkle with the flaked almonds and confectioners' sugar, and place under the hot broiler for a few seconds to caramelize the sugar.

Presentation
Spoon a little of the coulis onto 4 warmed plates, and place the fondants in the center. Scatter a few passion fruit seeds and a few slivers of pistachio, if desired, over the top.

Warm Baked Figs with Lime Syrup
and Raspberry Coulis

Serves 4

6 limes

²/₃ cup sugar

8 ounces raspberries

8 large attractive figs

1¹/₂ tablespoons unsalted butter, softened

Preparation

1   To make the lime syrup, scrub the limes under hot water, and dry thoroughly. Grate the zest of 4 of the limes, and peel off strips of zest from the other 2 with a swivel peeler. Carefully trim off and discard the white pith from the underside of the zests, and cut them into the finest possible julienne. Set aside.

2   Peel 2 of the limes completely, removing all the pith, and cut into segments between the membranes. Set aside.

3   Squeeze the other 4 limes to obtain a scant ¹/₂ cup of juice. Strain through a sieve into a saucepan, add ¹/₂ cup of the sugar, and bring to a boil, skimming the surface. Simmer to make a very thick syrup. Add the grated lime zests, and set aside.

4   Reserve a few raspberries for decoration. To make the coulis, purée the rest with all but 2 teaspoons of the remaining sugar in a blender or food processor. Press the coulis hard through a fine sieve to eliminate the seeds, and keep cool.

5   Cut off the hard stem of the figs. Make a cross in 4 of the figs, cutting halfway down the flesh. Quarter the remaining figs. Generously butter a flame proof baking dish, arrange all the figs in the dish, and set aside.

Finishing Touches

1   Preheat the oven to 400°F.

2   Sprinkle the figs lightly with the 2 teaspoons sugar, and bake in the hot oven for 4 minutes.

3   Remove the figs, set the dish over high heat, deglaze with the lime syrup, then add the julienne of zests.

Presentation

Place a generous spoonful of raspberry coulis in the center of 4 plates. Place a whole fig on top, and surround it with 4 fig quarters. Drizzle the lime syrup and julienne over the figs, and decorate with the reserved raspberries.

Warm Pineapple Meringue with Quinces and Toasted Almonds

Serves 4

5 quinces

2 cups granulated sugar

10 figs

1 pineapple

2 tablespoons unsalted butter

3 tablespoons maraschino liqueur

4 ounces puff pastry (page 201)

$^{1}/_{4}$ cup egg whites

$^{1}/_{2}$ cup flaked almonds

Confectioners' sugar

4 quenelles of Almond Milk
   Ice Cream (page 160)

Skinned pistachios, for garnish

Preparation

1   Preheat the oven to 425°F.

2   Peel the quinces, and cut them into $^{1}/_{4}$-inch dice. Put 1 cup water and $1^{1}/_{4}$ cups of the granulataed sugar in a saucepan, and bring to a boil, skimming the surface. Add the quinces, and simmer gently until tender; watch carefully, as they are delicate and cook quickly. Drain and set aside. Reserve some syrup for the garnish.

3   Peel 9 of the figs, and cut into $^{1}/_{4}$-inch dice. Cut the last one into thin slices. Peel the pineapple, quarter it lengthwise, remove the fibrous core, and cut the flesh into $^{1}/_{4}$-inch dice.

4   Heat the butter in a nonstick skillet, add the diced pineapple, and cook until the juices evaporate. Add sugar according to the ripeness of the pineapple, then deglaze with the liqueur, add the diced quinces and figs, remove from the heat, and stir together gently.

5   Roll out the puff pastry to a thickness of $^{1}/_{12}$ inch, and use it to line 4 oval tartlet tins. Refrigerate for 15 minutes, then bake blind in the hot oven for 10 minutes. Set aside.

Finishing touches

1   Preheat the oven to 400°F.

2   To make the meringue, beat the egg whites, adding $^{1}/_{4}$ cup of the granulated sugar, a little at a time. When the mixture has doubled in volume, add the remaining sugar, and whisk until the meringue is very firm, glossy, and smooth.

3   Fill the tartlet cases with the fruit mixture.

4   Using a spatula, spread the meringue over the fruits, then use a piping bag to pipe on little points.

5   Stick the flaked almonds into the meringue (see photo), sprinkle with the confectioners' sugar, and place the tartlets on a baking sheet lined with parchment paper.

6   Bake in the hot oven for 8 to 10 minutes.

Presentation
Unmold the tartlets, place 1 at the top of each plate, and put a quenelle of ice cream in the center of the plate. Garnish the top right-hand side with thin slices of fig, some pistachios, and a few drops of syrup.

Pistachio Soufflé

Serves 2 (This soufflé cannot be made successfully in larger quantities, so make two separate soufflés for 4 people.)

Sauce

Scant ¹/₂ cup crème anglaise
  (page 195)

2 teaspoons pistachios, skinned

1 drop bitter almond essence

5 drops kirsch

2¹/₂ tablespoons pistachios, skinned

5 tablespoons sugar

1¹/₂ tablespoons unsalted butter,
  softened

1 egg yolk

2 egg whites

Preparation

1 To make the sauce, prepare the crème anglaise, add the pistachios, almond essence, and kirsch, and pulse in a blender until smooth. Set aside.

2 Reserve 5 of the pistachios for the garnish. Grind the rest with 2¹/₂ tablespoons of the sugar in a spice or coffee grinder, and set aside.

3 Cut the reserved pistachios into slivers, and set aside.

4 Butter a straight-sided soufflé dish, and refrigerate.

Cooking

1 Preheat the oven to 450°F and place a shelf in the lowest position.

2 To prepare a bain-marie, pour about 1¹/₂ inches of water into a roasting pan, set over low heat, and keep at just below the boiling point.

3 Put the egg yolk in a bowl, and whisk in the ground pistachio and sugar mixture until very frothy.

4 Slowly beat the egg whites with the remaining 2¹/₂ tablespoons sugar, aerating them well; they should not be too stiff.

5 Using a whisk, stir one-third of the egg whites into the egg and pistachio mixture. Fold in the rest of the whites gently with a spatula, lifting the mixture and turning the bowl as you go.

6 Pour the mixture into the soufflé dish; it should not go all the way to the top.

7 Immerse the soufflé dish in the bain-marie, and cook at just below the boiling point, for 6 to 8 minutes. Transfer the soufflé dish to the bottom of the oven, and cook for about 12 minutes more. Sprinkle the flaked pistachios over the surface halfway through.

Presentation
Bring the soufflé to the table in the dish, and serve the sauce in a sauceboat. Divide the soufflé between 2 plates, and pour a thin ribbon of sauce around.

186

Lime Soufflé

Preparation

1 Scrub the lime and lemon under hot water, and dry thoroughly. Grate a little of the lime and lemon zest, and reserve the zest.

2 Butter a straight-side soufflé dish, and refrigerate.

3 To make the sauce, squeeze the lime and lemon, reserve 1 tablespoon of the juice, and strain the rest through a sieve into a saucepan. Add a scant $^1/_2$ cup of the sugar, and simmer to a syrup. Set aside.

Cooking

1 Preheat the oven to 500°F and place a shelf in the lowest position.

2 To prepare a bain-marie, pour about $1^1/_2$ inches of water into a roasting pan, set over low heat, and keep at just below the boiling point.

3 In a bowl, whisk the egg yolk with $2^1/_2$ tablespoons of the sugar and a small pinch each of the reserved lime and lemon zest, until very frothy. Stir in the reserved tablespoon of juice.

4 Slowly beat the egg whites with the remaining sugar, aerating them well; they should not be too stiff.

5 Using a whisk, stir one-third of the egg whites into the egg mixture. Fold in the remaining whites gently with a spatula, lifting the mixture and turning the bowl as you go.

6 Pour the mixture into the soufflé dish; it should not go all the way to the top.

7 Immerse the soufflé dish in the bain-marie, and cook at just below the boiling point, for 6 to 7 minutes. Transfer the soufflé dish to the bottom of the oven, and cook for no longer than 7 minutes.

Serves 2 (This soufflé cannot be made successfully in larger quantities, so make two separate soufflés for 4 people.)

1 lime

1 lemon

$1^1/_2$ tablespoons unsalted butter, softened

Scant 1 cup sugar

1 egg yolk

2 egg whites

Presentation
Bring the soufflé to the table in the dish, and serve the sauce in a sauceboat. Divide the soufflé between 2 plates, and pour a thin ribbon of sauce around.

Orange and Chocolate Meringue Sablés

Serves 4

Pâte Sablé
1/4 cup unsalted butter
1/4 cup confectioners' sugar
Pinch of salt
1 egg
1 egg yolk
1 cup all-purpose flour

Orange Filling
8 oranges, plus 1 or 2 for juicing
1 cup plus 3 1/2 tablespoons sugar
5 tablespoons Grand Marnier
2 tablespoons grenadine
4 ounces kumquats
2/3 cup fresh orange juice
4 ounces pineapple, peeled
4 teaspoons unsalted butter

Ganache
4 ounces bittersweet chocolate
    (70 percent cocoa solids)
Scant 1/2 cup whipping cream

Meringue
1/3 cup egg whites
2/3 cup sugar
Cocoa powder, for dusting

Presentation
Place a sablé in the center of each plate, and decorate artistically with the reserved orange syrup and the rest of the ganache.

Preparation

1   Preheat the oven to 400°F.

2   To make the pâte sablé, cut the butter into small pieces, put in a bowl, and mash with a wooden spoon until pliable. Add the confectioners' sugar, mix until completely incorporated, then do the same with the salt, whole egg, egg yolk, and flour, stirring each time to incorporate each ingredient before adding the next.

3   Roll out the pastry to a thickness of about 1 1/4 inches. Using a 1 1/2-inch pastry cutter, cut out 4 circles. Place on a baking sheet lined with parchment paper, and bake in the hot oven for about 10 minutes, until pale golden. Transfer to a wire rack, and leave to cool.

4   To make the orange filling, peel the 8 oranges, removing all the pith. Holding the oranges over a sieve set in a bowl, cut out the segments between the membranes, and put them in a small bowl. Measure the juice, and top it up to 2/3 cup by squeezing another 1 or 2 oranges. Put a scant 1/2 cup of the sugar in a small, heavy saucepan, and cook over medium heat until you have a light brown caramel, then deglaze with the 2/3 cup orange juice, the Grand Marnier, and the grenadine. Reduce by one-third over low heat, pour over the orange segments, and leave to infuse for 4 or 5 hours. Cut the infused orange segments into three pieces each.

5   Pour the cooked orange juice into a small saucepan, and reduce to a syrupy consistency. Reserve this syrup for decorating the plates.

6   Quarter the kumquats, and remove the seeds. Combine the 2/3 cup fresh, uncooked orange juice and a scant 1/2 cup sugar in a small saucepan, and bring to a boil. Add the kumquats, stir to mix, and cook gently for 6 minutes; the kumquats should still be slightly firm. Drain in a sieve, leave to cool completely, then cut into 1/4-inch dice.

7   Cut the pineapple into 1/8-inch dice. Heat the butter in a nonstick skillet, add the 3 tablespoons sugar and the pineapple, and cook, stirring constantly, until the pineapple is an even golden brown. Add the kumquats and the orange segments, cook for 1 or 2 minutes more, then drain in a sieve.

8   To make the ganache, break the chocolate into pieces, melt in a bain-marie over barely simmering water, and stir in the cream. Let cool slightly.

Finishing Touches

1   Put 1 tablespoon of the fruit mixture onto each sablé, add 1 teaspoon of ganache, and repeat, heaping the filling into a mound. Refrigerate for 20 minutes.

2   Preheat the oven to 475°F.

3   To make the meringue, put the egg whites and half of the sugar into a bowl, and beat until the egg whites have doubled in volume. Add the remaining sugar and continue to beat until the meringue is firm, glossy, and very smooth. Put it into a piping bag fitted with a no. 4 nozzle. Starting at the base, cover the dome of fruit with points of meringue, piped very closely together. Place the sablés on a baking sheet lined with parchment paper.

4   Dust the meringue lightly with cocoa powder.

5   Cook the sablés in the hot oven for 5 minutes.

Warm Souffléed Strawberry Soup

Serves 4

1 lime
1¹/₄ pounds strawberries
Scant 1 cup granulated sugar
3 eggs
1 tablespoon *sureau* (elderberry) syrup
Confectioners' sugar

Preparation

1   Scrub the lime under hot water, dry thoroughly, and peel off strips of zest with a swivel peeler.

2   Wash, hull, and drain the strawberries. Reserve 4 for the garnish, and cut the rest lengthwise into 6 pieces. Place in a bowl, and add ¹/₄ cup of the granulated sugar and the lime zests. Leave to macerate for 1 hour.

Finishing Touches

1   Preheat the oven to 400°F.

2   Remove the lime zest, and divide the strawberries and the juice they have rendered between 4 ovenproof bowls.

3   Separate the eggs, and put the yolks and whites in separate bowls.

4   Whisk the yolks with a scant ¹/₂ cup of the granulated sugar until very pale and frothy. Add the *sureau* syrup, and whisk.

5   Beat the egg whites with the remaining sugar until very soft peaks form; they should not be too stiff.

6   Scoop the whites onto the yolks, and fold them in delicately, lifting the mixture and turning the bowl as you go.

7   Put the mixture into a disposable paper piping bag, and snip off the end on the diagonal. Starting at the edge of the plate, pipe large, wide commas, making them narrower towards the center.

8   Dust with confectioners' sugar, and place in the top of the oven until slightly golden, watching carefully that they do not burn.

Presentation
Set each of the bowls on top of a chilled plate. Garnish
the center of the soufflés with sliced strawberries.

Basic Recipes

Herb Butter

Makes ¹/₂ cup

1 cup fresh chives; ¹/₂ cup parsley leaves; Scant ¹/₂ cup butter, softened; ground cayenne pepper; salt; freshly ground pepper

Preparation

1 Snip the chives and parsley.

2 Put the herbs and butter in an electric stand mixer, and blend until smooth and creamy.

3 Season to taste with cayenne pepper, salt, and pepper, and blend quickly.

4 Press the herb butter through a fine sieve, and store in the freezer until needed.

Vegetable Bouillon

Makes about 4 cups

1 leek, 1 large carrot, ¹/₂ celeriac (celery root), 1 large onion, 2 shallots, 6 cloves garlic, 1 clove, 1 bouquet garni (fresh thyme, parsley, and bay leaf), 4 cups water, 4 cups white wine, sea salt, coarsely crushed peppercorns

Preparation and Cooking

1 Peel the leek, carrot, celeriac, onion, and shallots, and cut into pieces. Halve the garlic. Stick the clove into a piece of onion.

2 Put all the ingredients into a stockpot, and cook gently for 1 hour, stirring occasionally.

3 Strain the stock through a fine chinois or a sieve lined with damp muslin or doubled cheesecloth.

4 Ladle the stock into small containers, and store in the freezer.

Chicken Stock or Bouillon

Makes about 10 cups

1 onion; 1 leek; 1 stalk celery; 1 clove; 1 clove garlic, crushed; 1 large chicken; some chicken giblets; 1 bouquet garni (fresh thyme, parsley, and bay leaf); 4 cups water, salt

Preparation and Cooking

1 Wash all the vegetables, peel as necessary, and cut into pieces. Stick the clove into a piece of onion.

2 Put the chicken and giblets in a stockpot, add the water, and bring to a boil, skimming the surface.

3 Add the vegetables and bouquet garni, and cook very gently for 2 hours, skimming the surface frequently.

4 Carefully lift out the giblets and chicken (reserve the meat for another use).

5 Strain the stock through a fine chinois or a sieve lined with damp muslin or doubled cheesecloth.

6 Leave to cool, then season lightly with salt.

7 Ladle the stock into small containers, and store in the freezer.

Chicken Consommé

Preparation and Cooking

1   Peel the vegetables as necessary, and chop them coarsely.

2   To make the clarification, put the egg whites in a large bowl, and whisk lightly just to break them down. Add all the vegetables, the thyme, peppercorns, and ice cubes.

3   Bring the chicken bouillon to a boil, and gently pour in the clarification, slowly stirring down to the bottom of the saucepan with a slotted spoon to move the clarification around.

4   Continue stirring and moving until the bouillon comes back to a boil, then simmer it very gently for 30 minutes. Use a ladle to make a hole in the surface at the point where the bubbles appear strongest. From time to time, ladle out some of the bouillon, and use it to moisten the surface of the vegetables.

5   After the 30 minutes is up, remove the pot from the heat, and leave the consommé to cool for 15 minutes.

6   Strain the consommé through a sieve lined with damp muslin or doubled cheesecloth.

7   Ladle into small containers, and store in the freezer.

Makes 10 cups

Clarification
1 leek, 1 carrot, 1 stalk celery, 1 tomato, 2 stalks parsley, 10 egg whites (not too fresh), pinch of thyme, pinch of coarsely crushed white peppercorns, 8 ice cubes

10 cups chicken bouillon (page 194)

Crème Anglaise

Preparation and Cooking

1   Combine the eggs, yolks, and sugar in a bowl, and whisk until pale.

2   Place the milk and vanilla bean in a saucepan, and bring to a boil. Pour the boiling milk over the egg mixture, whisking constantly.

3   Pour the mixture back into the saucepan and cook very gently, stirring with a wooden spoon until the sauce is thick enough to coat the back of the spoon. Take great care not to let it boil.

4   Pour the crème anglaise into a bowl and leave to cool, stirring occasionally to prevent a skin from forming.

Makes 2¹/₂ cups

2 eggs, 3 egg yolks, 1 cup sugar, 1³/₄ cups milk, ¹/₂ vanilla bean

Lamb Stock

See the recipe for veal stock on page 197, replacing the veal trimmings with lamb trimmings.

Lobster Stock

Preparation and Cooking

1 Remove the little sacs from high inside the lobster shells, as these will give the stock an unpleasant flavor. Chop the shells with a heavy knife, then pulse them in a food processor.

2 With the motor of the food processor still running, mix in the softened butter.

3 Peel and chop the garlic and shallots.

4 Heat the oil in a shallow pan, add the chopped shells and butter mixture, and cook until golden, stirring with a wooden spoon.

5 Add the garlic and shallots, lemon zest, parsley, thyme, and bay leaf, and cook gently for 2 minutes.

6 Quarter the tomatoes, add them to the pan, and cook until they begin to color.

7 Deglaze with the Cognac, and stir in the wine and fish stock.

8 Bring to a boil, skimming the surface, and simmer for 20 minutes.

9 Season the lobster stock with cayenne, salt, and pepper and pass it through a vegetable mouli, or strain through a fine sieve, pressing to extract the maximum flavor, and leave to cool.

10 Ladle the stock into small containers, and store in the freezer.

Makes 1³/₄ cups

4 lobster shells; ¹/₄ cup unsalted butter, softened; 3 cloves garlic; 2 shallots; 2 tablespoons extra virgin olive oil; 1 piece of lemon zest, 2¹/₂ by 1¹/₄ inches; 6 stalks parsley; 1 sprig thyme; 1 bay leaf; 2 tomatoes; ¹/₄ cup Cognac; ¹/₂ cup white wine; 1¹/₄ cups fish stock (page 198); ground cayenne pepper; salt; freshly ground pepper

Game Stock

Preparation and Cooking

1 Cut the venison trimmings into small pieces.

2 Heat 2 tablespoons oil in a large saucepan, add the venison and calf's foot, and fry briskly, stirring so that the meat does not stick to the bottom of the pan.

3 When the bones are well browned, add the bouquet garni, and cook, stirring, until the vegetables have browned. Scoop everything into a colander to drain off the fat.

4 Return it all to the saucepan, and pour in the water. Bring quickly to a boil, skimming the surface, then decrease the heat, and simmer gently for 1 hour.

5 Strain the stock through a fine chinois into a clean saucepan, set over high heat, and reduce to ¹/₄ cup.

6 Season and leave to cool. Ladle the cold stock into small containers, and store in the freezer.

Makes 2 cups

1 pound venison trimmings; 2 to 3 tablespoons peanut oil; 1 calf's foot, cut into chunks; 1 bouquet garni (fresh thyme, parsley, bay leaf, carrot, and leek); 4 cups water; salt; freshly ground pepper

Langoustine Stock

Preparation and Cooking

1 Clean the langoustine heads, and chop them with a heavy knife.

2 Put all the ingredients in a saucepan, bring to a boil, skimming the surface, and cook gently for 20 minutes.

3 Strain through a fine chinois or a fine sieve lined with damp muslin or doubled cheesecloth.

4 Leave to cool.

5 Ladle the cold stock into small containers, and store in the freezer.

Makes about 1¹/₄ cups

1 pound langoustine heads (keep them in the refrigerator until you have collected enough); 1 cup white mirepoix (mixed celery, onion, and white part of a leek, cut into ¹/₄-inch dice); ¹/₄ cup white wine; ³/₄ cup fish stock (page 198); 1¹/₄ cups water

Scallop Stock

Preparation and Cooking

1 Carefully wash the scallop beards under cold running water.

2 Peel and finely chop the shallots and garlic. Place in a saucepan with the butter, and cook over medium heat until the shallot is translucent. Add the scallop beards, and stir.

3 Pour in the bouillon and wine, add the bay leaf, parsley stalks, and peppercorns, bring to a boil, skimming the surface, then simmer gently for 20 minutes.

4 Strain through a fine conical sieve or a fine sieve lined with damp muslin or doubled cheesecloth.

6 Leave to cool. Ladle the cold stock into small containers, and store in the freezer.

Makes about 1 cup

Beards of 12 scallops, 2 shallots 1 clove garlic, 1½ tablespoons unsalted butter, 1¼ cups vegetable bouillon (page 194), ¼ cup white wine, 1 bay leaf, 5 stalks parsley, 5 peppercorns

Brown Veal Stock

Preparation and Cooking

1 Peel the garlic cloves, leaving them whole. Peel and dice the carrot, shallot, and onion.

2 Heat the oil in a large skillet until very hot, put in the veal bones and trimmings, and brown over very high heat, stirring constantly to prevent them from sticking to the bottom of the skillet.

3 When the bones are well browned, add the vegetables and bouquet garni, brown for a few minutes, still stirring constantly, then scoop into a colander to drain off the fat.

4 Scoop everything into a stockpot and pour in enough cold water (about 6 cups) to cover the bones generously. Add the tomato paste and salt, and quickly bring to a boil, skimming the surface.

5 Lower the heat, and simmer the stock for about 3 hours, adding water if necessary to keep the bones covered.

6 Strain the stock through a chinois or fine sieve into another saucepan, and reduce until only 4 cups of stock remain.

7 Leave to cool. Ladle the cold stock into small containers, and store in the freezer.

Makes 4 cups

2 cloves garlic; 1 large carrot; 1 large shallot; 1 large onion; 3 tablespoons peanut oil; 3 pounds veal bones, chopped; 1 pound lean veal trimmings, cut into small pieces; 1 large bouquet garni (fresh thyme, parsley, bay leaf, and leek); 1 heaping tablespoon tomato paste; 1 level tablespoon Kosher salt

Brown Chicken Stock

Preparation and Cooking

1 Chop the carcasses and gizzards with a heavy knife. Heat the oil in a saucepan until very hot, and brown the carcasses and gizzards over high heat, stirring to prevent them from sticking to the bottom of the pan.

2 Add the mirepoix and bouquet garni, and stir until slightly browned, then scoop the contents of the pan into a colander to drain off the fat.

3 Return everything to the saucepan, add the tomato paste, and pour in enough water (about 4 cups) to cover the bones and vegetables.

4 Bring to a boil, skimming the surface, then decrease the heat, and simmer for 2 hours, adding more water if necessary to keep the bones covered.

5 Strain through a chinois or fine sieve into a clean saucepan, and reduce to 2 cups. Season with salt and pepper.

6 Leave to cool. Ladle the stock into small containers, and store in the freezer.

Makes about 2 cups

1¹/₂ pounds chicken carcasses and gizzards; 2 tablespoons peanut oil; 1 cup mirepoix (mixed carrot, onion, and celery, cut into ¹/₄-inch dice); 1 bouquet garni (fresh thyme, parsley, bay leaf, and leek); ¹/₄ cup tomato paste; salt; freshly ground pepper

Fish Stock or Fumet

Preparation and Cooking

1 Rinse the fish bones thoroughly under running water, then cut into large pieces.

2 Place in a saucepan with the wine and water, and bring gently to a boil, skimming the surface frequently.

3 Stick the clove into the onion, and add it to the pan, together with the bouquet garni and bay leaf, and cook gently for 20 minutes.

4 Strain the stock through a fine chinois or a fine sieve lined with damp muslin or doubled cheesecloth.

5 Leave to cool. Ladle the cold stock into small containers, and store in the freezer.

Makes 2 cups

2 pounds sole and turbot bones; 2 cups white wine; 2 cups water; 1 clove;1 onion, peeled;1 bouquet garni (leek, carrot, celery, and fresh parsley); 1 bay leaf

Clear Gelée

Preparation and Cooking

1 Put the rounds of calf's foot in a saucepan, cover generously with cold water, and slowly bring to a boil. Drain, and refresh the calf's foot in ice water.

2 Put the calf's foot in a stockpot, pour in 8 cups cold water, and slowly bring to a boil, skimming the surface. When the water boils, add the bouquet garni, and simmer gently for 3 hours, adding more water when necessary to keep it at the same level.

3 Strain the stock through a fine sieve into a clean saucepan, and leave to cool completely.

4 To make the clarification, put the egg white in a bowl, and break it up lightly with a fork. Mix in the ground veal and the vegetables, and add a very little water to make a dense, slightly soft mixture. Add this to the cold stock, set the saucepan over high heat, and quickly bring to a boil, stirring continuously. As soon as the stock begins to boil, turn the heat down very low, and continue to cook for 30 minutes, skimming the surface from time to time.

5 Strain through a fine chinois or a fine sieve lined with damp muslin or doubled cheesecloth.

Makes about 4 cups

1 calf's foot, cut into rounds (have the butcher do this); 1 bouquet garni (fresh thyme, parsley, bay leaf, 1 carrot, and fresh leek)

Clarification
1 egg white; 7 ounces boneless shin of veal, coarsely ground; 1 carrot, peeled and chopped; 1 onion, peeled and chopped; white part of ¹/₂ leek, chopped; salt; freshly ground white pepper; wine

6 Leave the stock to cool, then remove the fat that rises to the surface.

7 Ladle the gelée into small containers, and store in the freezer.

8 Season the gelée just before using, and flavor with your chosen wine.

Fish Gelée

Preparation and Cooking

1 Combine the clear gelée and fish stock in a saucepan, set over high heat, and reduce by half.

2 In a bowl, lightly break up the egg white with a fork, add all the other clarification ingredients and a ladleful of the boiling reduction. Whisk lightly, and pour this mixture back onto the boiling reduction.

3 Decrease the heat, and cook gently for about 8 minutes. Make a hole in the vegetables to check if the jelly is crystal clear. When it is, strain it very carefully through a sieve lined with damp muslin or doubled cheesecloth, and leave to cool.

4 Ladle the cold gelée into small containers, and store in the freezer.

Makes about 2 cups

2 cups clear gelée (page 198), 2 cups fish stock (page 198)

Clarification
1 egg white; 1 tablespoon chopped celery; 1 tablespoon chopped leek; 1 tablespoon chopped carrot; 1 sprig lovage; 2 whole shrimp, chopped; 4 ounces fish fillet, chopped; scant 1/2 cup water

Red Wine Gelée

Preparation and Cooking

1 Heat the oil in a large saucepan, and lightly brown the veal shin and calf's feet. Add the bouquet garni, pour in the wine, and cook gently for 3 hours, topping up with water from time to time to keep the liquid at the same level.

2 Strain the resulting bouillon through a fine sieve, leave until cold, then return it to the saucepan.

3 To make the clarification, put the egg white in a bowl, and break it up lightly with a fork. Mix in the ground veal and vegetables, and add a very little water to make a compact, slightly soft mixture.

4 Add the clarification to the cold bouillon, and heat, gently at first, then increase the heat, and bring quickly to a boil, to bind the egg white. Turn the heat down as low as possible, and simmer gently for 20 minutes.

5 Pass through a fine sieve, leave to cool completely, and remove the fat that has risen to the surface.

6 Ladle the cold gelée into small containers, and store in the freezer.

Makes about 3 cups

1 tablespoon peanut oil; 1 shin of veal, cut into rounds; 2 calf's feet, cut into pieces; 1 bouquet garni (fresh thyme, parsley, bay leaf, small carrot, and white part of 1 leek); 8 cups full-bodied red wine

Clarification
1 egg white; 7 ounces boneless shin of veal, coarsely ground; 1 carrot, peeled and chopped; 1 onion, peeled and chopped; white part of 1/2 leek

Curry Oil

Preparation and Cooking

1 Cut the orange zest into small squares, and mix into the mirepoix.

2 Heat 1/4 cup of the oil in a saucepan, add the mirepoix, and cook until colored. Sprinkle on the curry powder and stir vigorously. Let the mixture scorch just slightly on the bottom of the pan, then add 3/4 cup of the oil, and cook very gently for 15 minutes.

3 Strain the oil mixture through a fine sieve, and add the remaining oil.

4 Pour the curry oil into a bottle, seal tightly, and keep in a cool place.

Makes about 1 3/4 cups

Zest of 1/2 orange, 1 1/4 cups mirepoix (mixed carrot, onion, and leek, cut into 1/4-inch dice), 2 cups peanut oil, 3 tablespoons strong Madras curry powder

Chile Oil

Preparation

Makes a scant ¹/₂ cup

2 ounces birdseye or serrano chiles,
scant ¹/₂ cup extra virgin olive oil,
1 leek, salt, freshly ground pepper

1 Cut off the chile stems, open them up, and carefully scrape out all the seeds. Finely chop the flesh with a little oil.
2 Trim the leek, pull off the 2 outside leaves, and shorten the green part by half. Wash well, and drain. Halve the 2 leaves lengthwise, lay them out flat on a chopping board, cut into very fine julienne, then into tiny dice.
3 Mix together the diced leek, chopped chiles, and the remaining oil, and season with salt and pepper.
4 Pour the chile oil into an airtight container, and store in a cool place.

Spiced Jus

Preparation and Cooking

Makes ²/₃ cup

Bones from 2 sole, 1 tomato,
1 tablespoon peanut oil, 1 cup
mirepoix (mixed carrot, celery, and
leek, cut into ¹/₄-inch dice), 1 level
tablespoon *ras-el-hanout* (North
African spice mixture), 1 tablespoon
tomato paste, ³/₄ cup full-bodied red
wine, ³/₄ cup fish stock (page 198),
1 bouquet garni (fresh thyme, parsley,
and bay leaf), ¹/₄ cup soy sauce

1 Wash the sole bones under running water, and cut into small pieces. Cut the tomato into large dice.
2 Heat the oil in a shallow pan, add the bones and mirepoix, and stir until lightly browned. Sprinkle on the *ras-el-hanout,* add the tomato and tomato paste, stir, and let scorch just slightly on the bottom of the pan before pouring in the wine and fish stock. Add enough water to cover everything, and bring to a boil, skimming the surface. Add the bouquet garni, and simmer for 30 minutes.
3 Strain the jus through a fine sieve into a clean saucepan, add the soy sauce, and reduce to ²/₃ cup.
4 Pour into an airtight container, and refrigerate.

Mixed Spice

Preparation

Makes about 1 cup

1¹/₂ tablespoons juniper berries,
3 tablespoons coriander seeds,
3 tablespoons freeze-dried pink
peppercorns, 1¹/₂ tablespoons
black peppercorns

1 Crush all the ingredients in a mortar.
2 Transfer to a food processor, and grind to a coarse powder.
3 Pack into an airtight container, and store in a dry place.

Italian Meringue

Preparation and Cooking

Makes about 2¹/₂ cups

³/₄ cup granulated sugar, ¹/₄ cup egg
whites, 1 tablespoon confectioners'
sugar

1 Cook the granulated sugar to the soft ball stage (240°F).
2 Whisk the egg whites with the confectioners' sugar until very firm.
3 Still whisking, gently pour the cooked sugar onto the egg whites in a steady stream, and continue to whisk until completely cold.
4 The meringue must be used immediately.

Puff Pastry

Preparation

1 Sift the flour into a bowl, add the diluted salt and softened butter, and knead gently for 3 minutes. Roll the pastry into a ball, flatten it between your hands, then wrap it in a damp cloth or plastic wrap, and leave to rest in the refrigerator for 2 hours.

2 After 2 hours, lightly flour the work surface, and roll out the pastry into a rectangle, about 8 inches long.

3 Cut the chilled butter into $1/8$-inch-wide slivers, and lay them on top of the pastry, leaving a $1/2$-inch border. Fold the pastry over the butter, and sprinkle it lightly with flour.

4 With the long side of the rectangle facing you, take the short end on the left-hand side, and fold one-third of the pastry into the middle.

5 Do the same with the right-hand side. You now will have made a rectangle with the short side facing you.

6 To make the first "turn," turn the pastry 45 degrees to the right, sprinkle it lightly with flour, and roll it into a rectangle three times its length. From now on, you will need to fold the rectangle into four, so mentally mark out the sections, 1, 2, 3, 4. Fold section 1 onto 2, and 3 onto 4, then close up the pastry like a book. You have now made a "double-turn". Brush off the flour, and refrigerate the pastry for 20 minutes.

7 Repeat step 6 to make a second double-turn. Always remember to turn the pastry 45 degrees to the right before making the next double-turn.

8 The pastry will be ready after two more double-turns (making a total of one single turn and four double-turns). Remember to brush off the flour and refrigerate the pastry for 20 minutes between each double-turn.

9 Divide the puff pastry into conveniently sized pieces, wrap these in plastic wrap, and store in the refrigerator or freezer.

Note: Making small quantities of puff pastry requires practice and manual dexterity, and a cold room to work in, so it is often better to buy a good quality, all-butter puff pastry from a reputable pastry shop.

Makes about $1^1/_4$ pounds

$2^1/_4$ cups all-purpose flour, plus extra for dusting; 1 teaspoon salt, diluted in 6 tablespoons water; $1/4$ cup unsalted butter, softened; $2^1/_4$ cups unsalted butter, chilled

Sweet Shortcrust Pastry

Preparation

1 Combine the flour, butter, sugar, and salt in an electric mixer fitted with the dough hook, and mix until the mixture resembles fine bread crumbs.

2 Add the egg and yolk and mix until the dough just comes together; this pastry must not be kneaded or over-worked.

3 Roll the pastry into a ball, wrap in plastic wrap, and leave to rest for several hours in the refrigerator before using. It will keep well for several days.

Makes 2 pounds

4 cups all-purpose flour; $1^1/_4$ cup chilled unsalted butter, diced; $1^1/_4$ cups sugar; pinch of salt; 1 egg; 1 egg yolk

Ravioli Dough

Preparation

1 Put the flour, salt, and 1 egg in an electric mixer fitted with the dough hook, and mix at low speed until the egg has been absorbed.

2 Add the second egg, mix until it has been absorbed, then add the third egg, gradually increasing the speed until the dough forms into a ball and comes away cleanly from the sides of the bowl. It should be firm, but elastic.

3 Wrap the ball of dough in plastic wrap, and leave to rest for 2 hours in the refrigerator.

Makes about 14 ounces

2 cups flour, pinch of salt, 3 small eggs (2 ounces each)

Viennese Pastry

Preparation

1 Cream the butter and sugar in an electric mixer.

2 Add the egg, and mix.

3 Fold in the flour, almonds, cinnamon, and lemon zest, and mix as gently as possible.

4 Wrap the pastry in plastic wrap, and refrigerate for at least 3 hours before using. It will keep in the refrigerator for 8 days, or you can cut it into several pieces, pack them in freezer bags, and store in the freezer for up to 3 months. Transfer the pastry to the refrigerator 24 hours before using.

Makes about 1¼ pounds

½ cup unsalted butter, at room temperature; 1 cup sugar; 1 very large egg; 2 cups flour, sifted; ¾ cup unskinned whole almonds, grated; ½ teaspoon ground cinnamon; ½ teaspoon grated lemon zest

Praline

Preparation

1 Oil a 10-inch diameter flan ring.

2 Heat the sugar in a saucepan over low heat, without stirring, until it begins to dissolve.

3 When the sugar has become liquid and pale golden, quickly stir in as many almonds and hazelnuts as the sugar will absorb. You must work very fast!

4 Pour the praline into the flan ring, and leave to cool and harden.

5 To use the praline, break off one or more pieces, and chop them with a knife just before using them in the recipe.

6 Store the praline in an airtight container in a dark place. You can also buy it ready-made from some bakeries.

Makes 1½ pounds

Grapeseed oil, for greasing; 3 cups sugar cubes; about 1½ cups unskinned whole almonds; about ½ cups unskinned whole hazelnuts

Saffron Rouille

Preparation

1 Steam the potato until tender, then press it through a very fine sieve into a bowl.

2 Soak the saffron in a little of the fish stock. Mix the egg yolk and saffron into the potato.

3 Pour in the two oils in a steady stream, whisking as if you were making mayonnaise. When the rouille becomes too thick, dilute it with a little more fish stock.

4 Season to taste with salt, pepper, a few drops of lemon juice, and a pinch of cayenne pepper.

Makes about 1³/₄ cups

2 ounces potato, peeled; pinch of saffron threads; ¹/₄ cup fish stock (page 198); 1 egg yolk; scant ¹/₂ cup extra virgin olive oil; ²/₃ cup peanut oil or other neutral-flavored oil; salt; freshly ground pepper; lemon juice; ground cayenne pepper,

Confit Tomatoes

Preparation and Cooking

1 Preheat the oven to 175°F.

2 Halve the tomatoes lengthwise, and remove the seeds. Arrange them on a baking sheet, skin-side down. Peel the garlic, slice it thinly, and place underneath the tomatoes.

3 Season with salt and pepper, sprinkle with thyme leaves, and dust lightly with the confectioners' sugar. Sprinkle with the olive oil, and cook in the oven for 1 hour.

4 Turn the tomatoes over, and cook for another hour.

5 Remove the baking sheet from the oven, leave the tomatoes until cold, then peel them, pack them with their oil and the garlic in an airtight jar, and keep in a cool place.

Makes 7 ounces

10 ounces Italian plum tomatoes, such as San Marzano; 1 clove garlic; salt; freshly ground pepper; leaves from 2 sprigs thyme; confectioners' sugar, for dusting; 2 to 3 tablespoons olive oil

Index

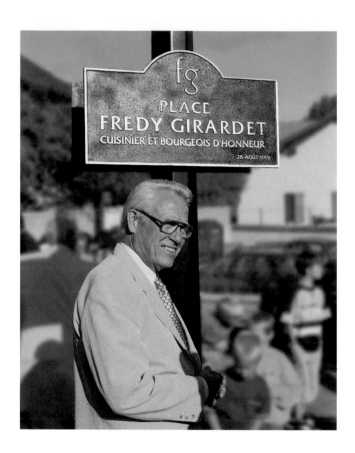

Acknowledgments

Frédy Girardet
would like to thank the following people for their kind help:

Gérard Cavascuns,
former head chef at Crissier

Adolf Blokbergen,
chef and director of l'Auberge du Raisin at Cully